in search of
TRUST

mastering trust in God

Thirtysix.org

A Search for Trust
Mastering Trust in God

ISBN 9781793003485

Published by:
Thirtysix.org
22 Yitzchak Road
Telzstone, Kiryat Yearim
Israel   90838

Nothing stands in the way of trust in God.

Leshem Shevo v'Achlamah

a search

SOME CONCEPTS ARE easy and some concepts are difficult. But then there are the concepts that are both easy AND difficult. They're easy to understand and figure out, but very difficult to actually implement. Trust in God falls into this category.

What's there to understand? Just TRUST in God. You don't know how you'll pay a bill? Don't worry, God will take care of it. You're having shalom-bayis problems? It's just a matter of time until God works it out. Can't solve a problem? God can, and will—so wait.

If only it were easier to trust in God! But then again, if it were, we wouldn't receive so much reward for it. If developing trust weren't so important, God would not have interfered in history and performed countless miracles to destroy Egypt and free the Jewish people. If it weren't so fundamental to Creation, then God would not be willing to undo it just because man chooses NOT to trust in Him.

So what's the problem? Why do we have such a tough time trusting in our Creator? Do we doubt His ability to give us what we need? Of course not! He's GOD. He can do ANYTHING, just by thinking about it.

Do we doubt that God WANTS to give us what we need? Hasn't He promised to do so many times in Tanach? Many times throughout our life, and throughout the millennia? Why make Creation with needs if You're not going to fulfill them?

So then why do we hold back? Why do we choose to rely on limited human beings rather than an unlimited God to take care of us, especially when THEIR success is dependent upon HIS will anyhow? Why don't we believe that God has our back?

Is it because we're not sure if God is really there? The Jews who witnessed the ten plagues, the splitting of the sea, and even the giving of the

Torah, CERTAINLY knew that God was there, and yet they too had a difficult time trusting in Him:

> Because you did not believe in God and did not trust in His salvation… (Tehillim 78:22)

> Nevertheless, they sinned further and had no faith in His wonders… (Tehillim 78:32).

Is it because God doesn't talk to us and tell us what He plans to do? Avraham spoke with God, and in the midst of actually hearing what God was planning to do, asked God for reassurance:

> He said to him, "I am God who brought you out of Ur Kasdim, to give to you this land as an inheritance."
> So he asked, "Lord God, how can I know that I will inherit it?" (Bereishis 15:7-8)

When Ya'akov Avinu dreamed of the heavenly ladder and was told to climb it, he refused—and we're still paying for that refusal:

> At that moment Ya'akov became afraid and said, "God forbid, just as these [angels] descended, I too will descend!"

The Holy One, blessed is He, said to him, "Do not be afraid, my servant Ya'akov. If you ascend, you will never descend."

However, he did not believe Him and would not ascend…"Nevertheless, they sinned further and had no faith in His wonders" (Tehillim 78:32)…[this] refers to our father Ya'akov, who did not believe and would not ascend. The Holy One, blessed is He, told him, "Had you believed in Me and ascended, you would never have descended. Now that you did not believe in Me and ascend, your children will undergo four exiles in this world in the future"… (Vayikra Rabbah 29:2)

Wow! These were great people, the GREATEST. And yet they too had difficulty with trust in God. Where does that leave us? And then there's this:

Moshe lifted up his hand with his staff and hit the rock twice; water came out in abundance. The people and their animals drank. God told Moshe and Aharon, "Since you did not believe in Me to sanctify Me before the Children of Israel, you will not bring this people into the land which I have given them." (Bamidbar 20:11-12)

Moshe Rabbeinu and Aharon HaKohen? If any two people had the ability to COMPLETELY trust in God, it would be those two. But they didn't. And we're supposed to? Are we supposed to be able to fly as well, WITHOUT wings?

On the other hand, even far simpler people have thrown their trust in with God, and have witnessed great miracles. Coincidence? Not when the Talmud states:

> No person stubs a finger if it is not first decreed Above. (Chullin 7b)

True, very true. But there was also the Holocaust, and thousands of years of pogroms before that. Undeniably God-trusting people suffered similar fates as those who didn't trust, which is one of the reasons it is so hard to trust in God with any real confidence. "They trusted," the yetzer hara says, "and look what happened to them!"

Probably one of the greatest to have ever trusted in God was Rebi Akiva. He not only died at the hands of the Romans, but in the worst way imaginable.[1] Indeed, he even died while saying the "Shema" with the greatest of intention! What

---

[1] Brochos 61b; Menachos 29b.

about those who race through it twice a day with minimal if any intention?

All good questions on this most important topic, which desperately needs intellectual and emotional clarity. Although many books have already been written to try to provide clarity, this one will be somewhat unique. Why? Because it is based on the teachings of someone who was VERY unique, Rabbi Shlomo Elyashiv, the "Ba'al HaLeshem," someone who clearly understood what it means to trust in God.

Rabbi Shlomo Elyashiv was born January 5, 1841, in Šiauliai, Lithuania. He made aliyah to Eretz Yisroel in 1924, where he died on March 13, 1926. He is called the "Ba'al HaLeshem," or just "the Leshem," after his works which he titled "Leshem Shevo v'Achlamah."[2]

The Leshem was a great kabbalist who had a vast knowledge of ALL aspects of Torah, and exceptional ability to clarify complicated concepts.

---

[2] The words are mentioned in Parashas Tetzaveh: "He made the Choshen…They filled it with four rows of stone…the third row: Leshem, Shevo, v'Achlamah" (Shemos 39:8-12). These words contain the letters of his name, "Shlomo."

It resulted in some of the most important kabbalistic works in the last few centuries.

The Chofetz Chaim[3] met with Reb Shlomo during his stay in Hamla, and commented that while our avodah is in this world, and we hope to achieve things in the higher worlds, Reb Shlomo, being so knowledgeable of the happenings in Heaven, "builds" there directly.

It is also known that the Chofetz Chaim said of Reb Shlomo that in this world it is still possible to stand next to him, but who knows if in the World of Truth it will be possible to stand in his realm. The Chazon Ish[4] said that Reb Shlomo was the last kabbalist. You can't get any better credentials than THAT.

All excepts from the Leshem are from his major work, titled "Drushei Olam HaTohu," Chelek 2, Drush 5, Anaf 4, Simanim 3-5.

---

[3] Rabbi Yisroel Meir Kagan (1839–1933), one of the Torah leaders of his time.

[4] Rabbi Avraham Yeshaya Karelitz (1878–1953), also one of the Torah leaders of his time.

A search for trust

אחת

Two Tracks

THE JEWISH PEOPLE had been enslaved for 116 years, ever since the last of Yosef's brothers, Levi, died.[1] As the Maharal explains, the Jewish people had been partially enslaved even before this time, but full-time slavery began with the death of Yosef's last brother.[2]

Moshe was born 36 years into the period of slavery, at the time the Egyptians were drowning male babies. Pharaoh's astrologers had told of the impending birth of a future savior and, unsure whether he would be Jewish or Egyptian, Pharaoh

---

[1] He died in 2332 from Creation.
[2] Gur Aryeh, Parashas Vayechi.

ordered that ALL male babies be thrown into the Nile River.[3]

To save the baby Moshe, Yocheved, his mother, hid him in a basket and set it afloat on the Nile River.[4] Moshe survived the journey and was soon found by Pharaoh's daughter, who raised him in the palace as her own son, right under Pharaoh's nose.[5]

This, however, did not stop Moshe from taking note of and feeling the burden of his own people.[6] Indeed, it was in defense of one Jew that Moshe killed an Egyptian taskmaster, forcing him to flee for his life when he was perhaps only 12 years old.[7]

In exile Moshe learned how to lead a people, eventually met his wife, and started a family.[8] That was also where he first met God at the burning bush, and received instructions to lead the Jewish nation to freedom and eventually to Eretz Yisroel.[9]

At the age of 79 and on behalf of God, Moshe

---

3 Rashi, Shemos 1:10.
4 Shemos 2:3.
5 Shemos 2:5.
6 Shemos 2:11.
7 Shemos Rabbah 5:1.
8 Shemos 2:15.
9 Shemos 3:7.

Rabbeinu took on the mightiest ruler of his time. Nine plagues and one year later, redemption was finally at hand. But as the Leshem explains:

> We find further that the Jewish people themselves were very surprised, as our rabbis say in Shir HaShirim Rabbah: When Moshe came and told the Jewish people, "in this month you will be redeemed," they said to him, "Moshe Rabbeinu, how can we be redeemed? All of Egypt is filthy from our idol worship!" (Shir HaShirim Rabbah, Parashah 2, Piska 8, Siman 2)

What was bothering the Jewish people? Redemption had been prophesied from the time of Yosef.[10] Moshe Rabbeinu had presented all the right credentials to be their redeemer, and had performed spectacular miracles to show just how capable he was with God backing him. What worried them?

Basically they told Moshe Rabbeinu, "Listen, there are only two ways to leave this place with its sealed borders. One way is with an army that is stronger than the Egyptians, which we clearly don't have, since we're now a slave nation. And

---

[10] Bereishis 50:24.

being Pharaoh's slaves, you can be sure he's not going to be excited about the idea of letting us go free, even for a few days. The other way is to need even BIGGER miracles to lead us out of the mightiest nation on earth, which means even BIGGER merits. Clearly we also don't have those, thanks to the idol worship we have been guilty of while living here."

Were they right? In normal times, yes. That's why until that time they had not gone out. That's why until that time they had remained slaves. But this was not a "normal" time :

> [Moshe] answered them, "Since He wants you to be redeemed, He does not look at your idol worship, but instead 'skips over mountains' (Shir HaShirim 2:8)."

Moshe Rabbeinu responded by saying essentially, "You're right. Your idol worship IS a big problem, and normally that WOULD definitely work against you. BUT—and this is the important part —God wants to redeem the nation and is therefore now prepared to overlook your sin of idol worship, like someone who 'skips over mountains' of sin!"

Sounds good. Since God was prepared to wipe their slate clean of the worst sin ever, even if only temporarily, who were they to complain? Why would they even want to complain? Since Moshe was sold on the idea, then shouldn't they be also?

The equation is simple: "keitz," a divinely designated time for redemption, means divine forgiveness. The only question is why. We're used to thinking that redemption is BECAUSE of merits, and that sins hold it back. We learn here that there are times when this just isn't true, and the question is why.

This is because all redemptions are the result of a revelation of "Arich Anpin."

This short sentence speaks volumes. First of all, it indicates that there is something very special and unique about redemptions in terms of Hashgochah Pratis—Divine Providence. Secondly, it opens a discussion about sefiros, the basis of all Kabbalah—and life for that matter.

Very briefly, sefiros are the divinely created spiritual system through which God filters His light and implements His will. Its source is called "Ohr Ain Sof—Light Without End." God's light is so spiritual that nothing else can exist within it, certainly not something physical or something that has free will. The sefiros, of which there are 10 general ones—Keser, Chochmah, Binah, Chesed, Gevurah, Tifferes, Netzach, Hod, Yesod, and Malchus—were created to solve that problem.

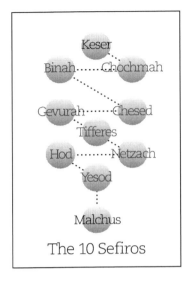

The 10 Sefiros

The basic role of a sefirah is to receive light from Above and reduce its spiritual intensity for the "worlds" below. By divine design the further down the light descends, the more "filtered" it becomes. And, the more FILTERED the light becomes, the more PHYSICAL it becomes, making Creation seem less godly and more random.

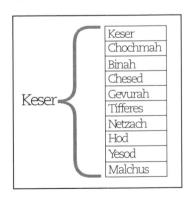

Just as there are 10 GENERAL sefiros, each sefirah also has its own subset of 10 sefiros, which have the same names as the original 10. When viewed in this manner, the sefiros are called "partzufim," literally "faces," and they gain other names: Arich Anpin, Abba, Imma, Zehr Anpin, and Nukvah, as follows:

Name of Sefirah	Name of Partzuf
10 sefiros of Keser	Arich Anpin
10 sefiros of Chochmah	Abba
10 sefiros of Binah	Imma
6 sefiros of Chesed to Yesod	Zehr Anpin
10 sefiros of Malchis	Nukvah

The "exception" here is "Zehr Anpin." Unlike the other partzufim, which are comprised of their own subset of 10 sefiros, Zehr Anpin actually consists of the six general sefiros of Chesed to Yesod. All the names have very specific meanings, especially with respect to their role in translating the will and light of God into components of Creation and history.

Therefore, when Moshe Rabbeinu told the Jewish people that the level of Divine Light being used to bring an end to their 116 years of slavery was that of Arich Anpin, he was actually explaining why they COULD leave Egypt, REGARDLESS of their spiritual shortcomings:

He explained to the Jewish people that the Holy One, blessed is He, was dealing with them on the level of the light of Arich Anpin called "Ayin," which works above any measure. In other words, it does not depend on merit or demerit.

In the Torah, specifically in the parshios of "Bechukosai" in Sefer Vayikra, and "Ki Savo" in Devarim, we are told about the rewards for following Torah, and the punishments for straying from it. The message is clear: Man can, through his actions, be his own best friend or his worst enemy. If he does right by God, he will bring blessing to his life. If he doesn't, HE is the one who causes God to ignore his needs and wants.

Yet the Jewish people were redeemed from slavery in Egypt without sufficient merit. They undeservedly crossed the sea on dry land and watched the pursuing Egyptians drown. Countless times throughout history GREAT miracles have happened for the Jewish people even though they didn't deserve them. How does THAT work?

The reason is that there are TWO tracks to history. One track is that of Zehr Anpin, which we control through our merits and demerits. We are empowered, but not to the point that we can destroy Creation. Our "Father" has given us great responsibility and decision-making authority to help run the "business," but not enough to irreversibly damage it.

This track of history operates from day to day. It's the history that happens IN BETWEEN redemptions, and which tends to HIDE God behind a veil that most call "nature." It's still ALL GOD, but in a covert and even somewhat deceptive manner. It is basically all cause and effect, which is why we, through our choices and actions, can play a role in history on this level.

This is also the reason the Jewish people did not break their bonds of slavery for 116 years. Technically they could have, had they built up enough merit to warrant leaving Egypt. Redemption might have happened in a far more mundane way, and it would certainly not have made the papers.

The second track of history is far different. It kicks in only when a "keitz" arrives. A keitz is divinely designated moment of redemption.[11] All of history is just to get to the Final Redemption which, as the Talmud points out, can happen in one of two ways: at the last possible time or at an earlier but propitious moment in history.

When a keitz comes along, it becomes the

---

[11] Sanhedrin 97b.

driving force in history. Things just start to "happen" to allow pieces to fall into place in order to fulfill the historical need of the keitz, if not fully, then at least partially.

Purim and Chanukah are the two most overt examples of this and, like the redemption from Egypt, both were quite miraculous for a good reason. Like all Jewish redemptions, they were the result of the light of Arich Anpin.

But isn't everything the result of the light of Arich Anpin at some point in time? Since the lower sefiros cannot get Divine Light if it doesn't first come through Arich Anpin, what is special about redemptions that we point this out, and that it makes these two holidays miraculous?

The answer is that, yes, everything at some point in the flow of Divine Light receives its light via Arich Anpin. But the more sefiros the light has to emanate through, the more filtered and less OBVIOUSLY miraculous, it becomes. ALL of life is a miracle, but most of it only covertly so, hidden behind a veil of consistency.

Redemptions, the Leshem is explaining, ARE the light of Arich Anpin, UNFILTERED. That huge and awesome miracle you witnessed? That's everyday business for the level of Arich Anpin. That incredible revelation of God you experienced? The light of Arich Anpin as well.

But being such a sublime level of Divine Light, it is beyond human impact. In fact, it is SO spiritual that, compared to the physical world, it is as if it doesn't even exist. This is why it is also called "Ayin," which generally means "nothing." But since it is so close to the original Source of light, the Ohr Ain Sof, it is far more "something" than anything below it.

It takes a keitz, however, to initiate its overt entry into human history and turn it upside down for the sake of some level of redemption. This is true on a personal level and even more so on a national level. This was only the FIRST lesson for the Jews of Egypt. The program had just begun, and there was still much to learn.

A search for trust

Just a Test

WE KNOW WHAT happened next. It's in the Torah. The Jewish people left Egypt that Nissan, as Moshe had foretold. That was after having been enriched by their former Egyptian taskmasters[1] and witnessing God Himself perform the final plague, the death of the firstborn.[2] The Jewish people had experienced the power of the light of Arich Anpin, and it had to have changed their lives.

Did they still worry? Yes:

---

[1] Shemos 12:35.
[2] Shemos 12:29.

However, they also knew well that without merit and good deeds, it would be impossible for this light to remain with them.

In other words, although it may not have taken merit for the light to come down and redeem them, they nonetheless thought that they needed merit in order to maintain access to that light. How could they possibly maintain the appropriate level of merit, when they had just left slavery behind and were about to travel through the desert?

This had been their concern at the BEGINNING of Jewish history. It will not be a concern at the END of it:

> In the future time, that is, in Yemos HaMoshiach, this light, that is not the result of merit or good deeds at all, will also be revealed, as it says (Yeshayahu 52:3), "You have sold yourselves for nothing, and you shall be redeemed without money"—without teshuvah or good deeds, as we have written in many other places.

What is the meaning of the words, "redeemed without money"? The Jewish people will not have to "pay" for redemption, not with teshuvah and not with good deeds. The light of Arich Anpin will emanate simply because the time for redemption will have come.[3] It will remain with them as well:

> At that time the revelation will be continuous because in the time to come the yetzer hara will be completely eliminated, as it says in Zechariah, "I will remove the spirit of impurity from the land" (Zechariah 13:2), and there will no longer be any free will. This is what the Ramban writes on Devarim 30:6, and merit and demerit will no longer be relevant, as our rabbis say (Shabbos 151b). At that time everyone will be completely righteous, like all the heavenly hosts that serve Him and do His will.

When the Jewish people left Egypt, they were just beginning their history as a nation. Clearly they still had a yetzer hara, and had yet to receive Torah. Free will was alive and well, which meant that they COULD choose to do that which merited the light of Arich Anpin on a permanent basis.

---

[3] The Talmud also discusses whether or not teshuvah and good deeds will be necessary for the Final Redemption (Sanhedrin 97b). But it is clear from the beginning of the discussion that it is referring to a non-keitz time.

When the Jewish people leave this fourth and last exile, that will be the end for this stage of history. As the prophet has foretold:

God will be king over the entire land. On that day God will be One, and His Name, One. (Zechariah 14:9)

This is another way of saying that the light of Arich Anpin at that time will be a worldwide event. The reality of God will become so palpable for EVERYONE living at that time that evil will be unable to exist any longer, resulting in the complete elimination of the yetzer hara and, along with it, free will.

Therefore the revelation of the light of Arich Anpin will be permanent then, unlike at the time of the redemption from Egypt, when the yetzer hara and impurity were not yet eliminated from the world at all. As a result, whether it [the light] remained or not was dependent on the actions of the Jewish people, as mentioned earlier at length in Section 2. As long as the yetzer hara is in the world, merit and demerit are possible, and He, may His name be blessed, rewards those who observe His mitzvos and punishes those who transgress them. If so, then it is not possible for the revelation of the light of Arich Anpin—which perseveres and overlooks the [deeds of the] rebellious and the good [alike], doing good for [both] evil and good people—to remain permanently revealed at this time.

The Jewish people therefore had made a valid point to Moshe Rabbeinu, as the Leshem continues:

Therefore it was about this that the Jewish people were constantly afraid and worried. The Holy One, blessed is He, had given them a taste of the revelation of this great light at the time of redemption and at the splitting of the Red Sea, and after that they came to the desert and constantly worried that the light would cease and that they would be judged according to their actions. Who could stand up to this judgment?

So far, redemption from Egypt and then from the pursuing Egyptian army required the light of Arich Anpin. And so far, they didn't have to do anything to warrant it. All they had to do was follow Moshe Rabbeinu wherever he took them.

They knew quite well, while standing at the

edge of a foreboding desert, that the need for miracles was not going to end there. On the contrary, they knew that they could survive in the desert only BECAUSE of ongoing miracles.

If they did not merit the light of Arich Anpin, then they would descend to the level of Zehr Anpin. That is the level of Divine Providence that rewards the obedient and punishes the wayward. How many of them would survive a deadly desert on THAT level? No wonder they panicked.

> This is what they meant by "Is God among us or not—ayin?" (Shemos 17:7), as we said at the beginning, based on the Zohar.

On a simple level, the Jewish people asking this question wanted to know if God had taken them that far and had since left them. Although it seems like a reasonable question from where we're standing, as Rashi points out, it led to the attack from what would become the greatest nemesis of the Jewish people (AND God), Amalek.

However, after hearing the Leshem's explanation about redemption and the light of Arich Anpin, which happens to also be called "Ayin," the question seems more profound. The question becomes "Is God among us or Ayin?" Are we on the Zehr Anpin track, where sins make a difference, or the Arich Anpin track, where they don't?

This is what the Zohar says: "[When] they came to the desert [to see the light of the glory of God], the Holy One, blessed is He, took His glorious light from there, etc. Rebi Shimon said, 'While they were still walking in the desert (immediately when they came to the desert) another "domain" of the rest of the nations was revealed to them, one which controls the desert (i.e., the Sitra Achra[4]). It met them (to instigate them, to lead them astray, to harass them through his machinations). The Jewish people saw that the glorious light of their King wasn't there, as it says, "They came to Marah, etc."'"[5] (Zohar, Beshallach 60a). See there. Thus even though they saw that the Clouds of Glory constantly surrounded them, they began to feel harassed by the Sitra Achra. It made them fear that perhaps the revelation of the light of Atika Kadisha[6] had ceased, and this why they

---

[4] The Sitra Achra is the ministering angel of Edom, Eisav's descendants, and the one whose role it is to encourage people to sin.

[5] Shemos 15:23.

[6] Literally, "Holy Ancient One," and another name for Arich Anpin.

asked, "Is God among us or Ayin?"

After all, how could such evil and impurity co-exist with such incredible holiness in the same place? The fact that they could sense the Sitra Achra, which meant that they felt their own yetzer hara, made them believe that the light of Arich Anpin had been withdrawn. This made them very nervous, so they asked about it.

It's important to recall that when we read stories like this, we're reading them AFTER the fact. We know how they end. We know what went on at the time. But they didn't. For them, everything was new, VERY new. They had to deal with the desert. WE do not.

Furthermore, they had to cope with going from slavery to freedom. WE don't. The nation at that time was TOTALLY reliant on others for survival and on God in particular, but we feel self-sufficient. They did not know what to expect, or what was expected of them...

But Moshe Rabbeinu knew quite well that this was to test them, and therefore he led them into the desert, which is the place of the Sitra Achra and his dominion, as it says in [the Zohar]: "It is the place of the Sitra Achra and his rulership, etc., in order to battle against his trickery, to break his power and strength, and to smash his head and humble him" (Parashas Tetzaveh 184a), as we mentioned above in Anaf 3, Siman 5.

It had all been a huge MISPERCEPTION. It had APPEARED to them as if they were beginning a journey into an extremely dangerous desert to confront the GREATEST enemy of them all, the SITRA ACHRA, without the help of the supermiraculous light to which they had been accustomed back in Egypt. They felt very much alone and very intimidated.

This feeling of aloneness could not have been farther from actual truth. They had not been at all alone, but rather in a test situation, to see how far they had already come spiritually and how far they were prepared to go. They had been set up by God, not to conspire against them but rather to test them.

Hashgochah Pratis, it turns out, had maneuvered the Jewish people into the position they found themselves in. It was designed to give them a special opportunity to do something important, something that would have changed them and Jewish history forever.

Did they get it?

Did they fail?

Is the message still relevant to us?
The Leshem answers all this too.

A search for trust

three
Journey to Trust

WHAT IS THE goal of life? What are we RE-ALLY here to accomplish? Life can be so very complex and confusing that it completely distracts us from our true purpose. People may THINK they're on track in life when in fact they've strayed totally from its main goal.

The exodus from Egypt was not only about leaving slavery. In fact, it was first and foremost an education in how to live life to its fullest, and everything that happened along the path to freedom was to TEACH the Jewish people specifically how to do this.

At the edge of the desert and feeling the influence of the Sitra Achra, they had to quickly figure out what it was God wanted them do, in order to master their situation rather than becoming slaves to it. This is what that meant:

> Had the Jewish people constantly strengthened themselves, so that their souls and hearts were given over to God, trusting in Him, may His name be blessed, that He would not remove the revelation of the great light of Atika Kadisha, also while they were in the desert…

What happened is subtle, but very, very important. Two little words entered their minds. Only TWO words, but two words that undermine the very basis of bitachon and emunah, trust and faith in God: "what if." WHAT IF it DOESN'T go as hoped…WHAT IF God DOESN'T come through for me…?". Just as we know how much we hope to succeed, we are usually also aware of how we can fail. That creates doubt.

It is no coincidence that the gematria of "Amalek" is the same as "suffek—doubt":

Ayin	70	Samech	60
Mem	40	Peh	80
Lamed	30	Kuf	100
Kuf	100		240
	240		

Amalek IS doubt in Hashgochah Pratis, making him the nemesis of God and the Jewish people, in whatever form "Amalek" takes. If something promotes doubt in God, it is Amalekian.

To go to war against Amalek therefore is to fight against doubt in Divine Providence. YES, things have gone terrible "wrong" in Jewish history. YES, there is something called "Hester Panim," the hiding of God's face from man:

> My fury will rage against them on that day, and I will ABANDON them and HIDE My face from them... (Devarim 31:17)

YES, this would seem like reason enough to ask the question, "What if ...?"

At least that is what Amalek argues, and uses our own yetzer hara to insidiously make his case. Those who are weak in trust in God often listen to it, allowing it to impact their decision about how act going forward. The Ba'al Bitachon ignores it, and proceeds as if the "what if?" doesn't even exist.

For example, a particular young man wanted to buy a house, but all he had was $10,000 for the down payment. Nevertheless, he decided to go through the process anyhow. He found a house he liked at a cost of $250,000, met with the builder, and made a deal. He had 30 days to come up with the balance, or he would lose not only the house but also the down payment, which was his entire savings.

He had no idea how he would come up with the balance of the money, but he had already come up with $84,000 when the builder arranged for that much of the mortgage to be transferred to his name. Within two days he had paid for 37% of the house, getting a mortgage he would have been denied had he just walked into the bank on his own, He was amazed.

However, he still had the lion's share of the amount to come up with, and only 30 days in which to do it. He knew he could count on his parents and in-laws for some of it, but not even most of it. He couldn't get another mortgage because he wouldn't have been able to pay it off even if he were able to get it. He and his wife just did not earn enough money to pay for two monthly mortgages.

"What if I can't raise the rest of the money?" he asked himself. "What if I lose my down payment...I'll have nothing left at all!"

Then he heard another voice that he did not recognize. It said, "But what if we DO come up with the rest of the money?"

"But how? Where?" the first voice asked with great skepticism.

"I don't know," the new voice answered. "but since God can do anything, He can do this too."

"I don't doubt that God CAN do such a miracle. I doubt that He WILL do such a miracle for us."

"Well," the new voice concluded, "I'm going to act as if He will."

"That's just reckless," the old, pessimistic voice argued. "What if ..."

"Nope!" the new voice cut him off. "I'm not going to deal with the 'what if.' I'm going a different route now. I'm going to simply say to myself, 'I can't wait to see how God will save the day!'"

That is exactly what he did, and God did His part as well. By the time the 30-day deadline arrived, he had all the money he needed to close the deal on the house. Both sets of parents helped out more than anticipated, and a friend unexpectedly lent him the difference.

As gratifying as it was to have been able to buy the house, a HUGE miracle he has never forgotten, he is even MORE grateful that he had pushed aside the negative "what if" and replaced it with a positive one. He had dared to dream, and his dream had come true. He could not help but conclude that his unrestricted trust in God had something to do with it.

We never lose when we trust in God. We only lose when we DON'T trust in Him, and that was the main message for the Jews leaving Egyptian slavery. It's the point of every test. It's what God is looking for in a believer.

> They should not have paid attention at all to the Sitra Achra and his schemes, because all of it was just a test. And this is specifically the kind of "awakening" from below necessary for drawing down and forever maintaining the revelation of the great light of Arich Anpin continuously.

Fear of failure is a real and powerful emotion, as is the fear of disappointment and pain. We go to great lengths to avoid them, including becoming as self-reliant as possible. It may not be the most responsible thing to do, but it certainly seems like the "safest."

In other words, people would rather believe in something they can see, even though it is limited in ability, than in something they cannot see, even if it is supposed to be UNLIMITED in ability. Being able to actually see something makes them feel as if the odds are more in their favor—even though they really are not.

But that's only because people do not take the time to know God better. They do not apply sufficient effort to learn how He works, or to appreciate what He has done and DOES DO on a moment-to-moment basis. Trust in anyone is commensurate to knowledge of them, to the point that we no longer have to see them in action to believe with confidence that they are looking out for our good.

What about all the bad things God has done to people, or at least let them happen? That's what makes God seem so unreliable in the minds of the non-trusting. How do the trusting people fit the bad things into their bitachon framework?

The truth is that bad things are the long-term result of when the Jewish people stopped trusting in God, and decided to rely more on themselves than on Him. The Torah explicitly states this in several places, when talking about the reward for following God, and the opposite for turning our backs on Torah. It's just that we expect God to act close to us at the same time that we live far away from Him.

Moshe Rabbeinu knew that the matter depended only upon them at that time, to strengthen their hearts in faith and trust in God. It is for this that the verse disparages them, "Because they did not believe in God and did not trust in His salvation." (Tehillim 78:22). It further says, "Nevertheless, they sinned further and had no faith in His wonders" (Tehillim 78:32).

Bitachon and emunah are not something a person just has. It is a level of relationship that like any relationship takes time to build. It is only natural to trust people, but only people we can naturally trust. God Himself acknowledged this when He said:

> You have been SHOWN, in order to KNOW that God, He is God; there is none else besides Him. (Devarim 4:35)

Thus the word "emunah," which means "faith," is like the word "uman," which is a craftsman. Professionalism is not something assumed, but something that is revealed over time through consistent expertise. It is the previously known successes that indicate if a person can be relied upon for future yet-to-be-seen successes.

In other words, emunah is about the past. Bitachon is the projection of it into the future. "I see that so-and-so has been FAITHFUL in the past. I TRUST that he or she will be faithful in the future."

That's what God was saying to the Jewish people. "You SAW what I did for you to bring you this far. You WITNESSED how I kept My promise and came back for you. You EXPERIENCED how I am willing to suspend the laws of Creation just to make you into a Torah nation. I have PROVEN Myself. Now it's up to you to project all of that into the future, YOUR future…in a place in which you can rely ONLY on Me to survive."

The Talmud recounts how Chizkiah HaMelech was decreed to die.[1] Yeshayahu told him so. However, Chizkiah told the prophet:

> I have a tradition from my father's house. "Even if a sharp sword rests upon a man's neck, he should not stop praying." This saying is also recorded in the names of Rebi Yochanan and Rebi Elazar: "Even if a sharp sword rests on a man's neck, he should not stop praying, as it says, 'Though He slay me, I will still trust in Him' (Iyov 33:15)." (Brochos 10a)

What the Talmud means is that, when it comes to God, salvation can come at the VERY LAST SECOND. Human beings do not have such control over life that they can take last-minute

---

[1] Brochos 10a.

risks and comfortably succeed. They need to leave room for error.

Not God, though. He has PERFECT control over EVERYTHING. For all we know, the solution is already in the works while we're still scrambling to find it. He's the One Who makes the antidote before the illness[2] because He controls both of them.[3] He sees things we can't, and if we would just give God His due, we would always find it quite natural to completely trust in Him for success at everything.

That's really the SECRET to bitachon. It's not about blindly trusting in God only when we have a tough time doing something. That counts too, but it doesn't usually last very long. It's about doing whatever we can to better KNOW God and how He works.

That was, in the end, what the exodus from Egypt was meant to accomplish. It wasn't just freedom from physical slavery. It was freedom from ignorance of God. The journey from Egypt to Sinai and then to Canaan was one of getting to know God well, so that by its end, we would realize that we can trust ONLY in God.

---

2 Megillah 13b.
3 Avodah Zarah 59a.

A search for trust

four

First Principle

IT IS NOT uncommon to project our own shortcomings onto others, and then blame them for what we lack. Ironically, this is the one of the biggest obstacles to achieving the all-important trait of bitachon. This, as the Leshem explains, was part of the problem for the Jews who left Egypt:

> However, all this was not because they had evil hearts, God forbid, but because they did not find themselves worthy of this.

If you had asked a Jew following Moshe Rabbeinu through the desert, "Why don't you trust in God for your well-being? Is it because you don't think God can take care of all your needs, or that He doesn't want to?" he or she would have answered, "God forbid! I know God can do ANYTHING He wants. And I know that God really WANTS to give me whatever I need. But I also know that a person requires sufficient merit for such divine assistance, and unfortunately for me, I just don't have it!"

This is the reasoning of the "Chassid" in "Chovos HaLevavos,"[1] Sha'ar HaBitachon, Ch. 3, Introduction 4: Only one who performs His will, may His name be blessed, the entire Torah and [all] mitzvos, and is a faithful servant of God can make use of the trait of bitachon.

We even say this in Shemonah Esrai, when we refer to God as "the support and trust of the RIGHTEOUS." Does this mean that someone who is NOT righteous—but who does trust in God—is really better off taking matters into his own hands, because God won't come through for him?

---

1 Duties of the Heart.

The Jews of Moshe's time thought so.

> Therefore, when they came to the desert and found themselves constantly tempted by the Sitra Achra and his trickery, they did not encourage themselves to trust in God, so that He would deal with them beyond measure and with constant miracles. They said that they were not worthy of this, and therefore constantly complained, "Why did you bring us up from Egypt, since it is impossible to properly maintain faith in God, may His name be blessed, because of the yetzer hara that gets stronger and is renewed each day?

If a person goes to a holy place, it is relatively easy to connect to God and remain connected. The yetzer hara is still with that person, but it is out of its element and has a more difficult time causing him or her to sin in any serious way.

But should that same person then enter an unholy environment, it is a completely different story. It will be MUCH harder for the person to connect to God. The yetzer hara will use the non-spiritual environment to constantly pull a person in a non-spiritual direction, eventually causing that person to sin.

This might not worry people very much if

they do not feel that they need God's help. They might notice their drop in behavior and feel somewhat uneasy about it, but they will not feel in danger because of it. They might even cut themselves some slack and rationalize their behavior.

But someone who, for example, is on an airplane when serious turbulence hits, recognizes the danger he is in and will start to pray or learn some Torah. Similarly, someone who happens to find himself in a dangerous neighborhood may start to worry about past sins. He certainly won't stroll along casually, as he wonders why God led him into danger.

The Talmud records the following discussion:

Rebi Chanina and Rebi Yonason were walking on a road and came to a fork. One path led by the door of a place of idol worship, and the other by a place of harlots. One said to the other: "Let's go by the place of idolatry, the inclination for which has been abolished."[2]

However, the other said: "Let's go by the place of the harlots, defy our inclination, and

2 Yoma 69b.

earn reward."

As they approached that place, they saw the harlots withdraw at their presence.

"How did you know this[3]?" he asked him.

He told him, "[The verse says,] 'Thought—mezimah—shall watch over you, and discernment will guard you' (Mishlei 2:11)."

The Rabbis asked Rava: "What does 'mezimah' mean? Let's say 'Torah,' since it writes 'zimah,' which is translated [by Onkeles] as 'COUNSEL of the wicked,' And it is written, 'Wonderful is His COUNSEL[4] and great His wisdom' (Yeshayahu 28:29)."

"If so, then 'zimah' should have been written.[5] This is what it means: 'Mezimah—from lewdness—Torah will protect you.'" (Avodah Zarah 17b)

In other words, divine protection requires merit, specifically Torah and mitzvos, which the people in the desert had yet to receive. Therefore they perceived themselves as being unworthy of such protection, and decided that God would not, COULD not help them. Who wouldn't think that

---

[3] That they would be protected from any solicitation.
[4] That is, Torah.
[5] And not "mezimah."

in a similar situation?

> With respect to this they erred greatly, making two mistakes. The first was [not believing] that the Holy One, blessed is He, does not play games with His creations, as the Talmud teaches (Avodah Zarah 3a).

If a person is spiritually careless, then he can find himself in situations that work against him. It can be a result of his own carelessness or God's desire to teach him to improve, but failure CAN be an inevitable result for such a person.

But if someone generally tries to do the right thing and yet finds himself in a potentially compromising situation, he has to know that this is only a test. The situation may SEEM impossible and failure may SEEM inevitable. But God would not have put him in such a situation if there weren't a way for him to succeed.

How should such a person respond?

> All a person can do is constantly strengthen himself, [as it says]: "One who comes to purify himself, [Heaven] helps him" (Shabbos 104a; Yoma 38b). [The rabbis] there are also reassuring: "If a person sanctifies himself a little, [Heaven] sanctifies him a lot."

This is a crucial point when it comes to bitachon and emunah. People give up hope when they are confronted with a situation they "know" they can't resolve, at least not on their own. They see the problem as all or nothing, even though the mishnah teaches:

> It is not incumbent upon you to complete the work, but neither are you at liberty to desist from it. (Pirkei Avos 2:16)

This means that we don't HAVE to be able to resolve a crisis on our own to solve it. We just have to be able to do SOMETHING about it, to make a concerted effort to fix the problem, no matter how ridiculously small that effort may seem. That is what Heaven needs to see before it makes up the balance of what we cannot provide.

It doesn't make a difference how big the problem is or how small our effort turns out to be. The approach is always the same: What can I RESPONSIBLY do to resolve the issue? The REST is God's business, not ours, what we call "Siyita d'Sh'mya," or "Heavenly Help."

When the Jewish people asked, "Is God among us or not?" God answered the question with an attack from Amalek. Why? Rashi answers this question as follows:

The Torah places this section immediately after this verse (when they asked, "Is God among us or not?") to imply that "I am always among you and ready at hand for everything you need, and yet you ask, 'Is God among us or not?' By your lives, that 'dog' will come and bite you, and you will cry out for Me, and then you will know where I am!" (Rashi, Shemos 17:8)

Rashi does not stop here though. He feels compelled to provide the analogy the Midrash uses:

This can be compared to a man who placed his son on his shoulder and set out on the road. Whenever his son saw something he wanted, he would say, "Father, take that thing and give it to me," and he would give it to him. They met a man along the way, and the son said to him, "Have you seen my father?" So his father said to him, "You don't know where I am?" He threw him down, and a dog came and bit him. (Tanchuma, Yisro 3; Shemos Rabbah 26:2)

There were probably several other more down-to-earth examples—literally—that the

Midrash could have used to make the same point. It is interesting that the one chosen places a son on top of his father's shoulders, extending the son's ability, so to speak.

On the other hand, if trust in God to make up for our shortcomings is the point, then the analogy is perfect. Aren't we the ones sitting on OUR Father's shoulders, accomplishing all that we do on a daily basis, forgetting that it is OUR Father Who is doing the work for us?

Everything we are, and all that we are able to do, is from God. And yet we act as if WE made ourselves, as if WE gave ourselves the wherewithal to succeed in life. What a delusion! It is always God doing our will, but from behind the scenes.

Forgetting this can lead to a rude awakening, once God decides enough is enough and gives us the opportunity to find out firsthand just how dependent on Him we really are. That's when the "dog," which has many forms, comes and nips at us.

If we could only realize how much God does come through for us every moment of every day, in situations in which it APPEARS as if we are easily working alone, then we would have no problem trusting in Him in those situations in which it APPEARS that we cannot possibly succeed on our own.

The entire world was created for this, with the evil and the good, to be rectified by man, and a person is not free from this work, as it is written: "As for what enters your minds— it shall not be!" (Yechezkel 20:32). See Sanhedrin 105a. It was with respect to this that the covenant was made, as it says in Tanchuma, Parashas Nitzavim, 3. See there, and the Sifri at the end of Parashas Shlach; see both places.

The verse from Yechezkel, quoted by the Talmud and the Midrash, is speaking about the desire of the Jews of that time to throw off their Torah responsibilities, to become like the people of the nations of the world. The prophet told them that it wasn't going to happen, because the covenant between God and the Jewish people was irreversible.

The world was created to be rectified by man. The Torah was given to the Jewish people to facilitate such rectification. But it is up to every individual to COURAGEOUSLY do whatever he or she can to make it happen, and to trust in God for the rest.

A search for trust

five
Second Principle

JUST TO RECAP, the first principle is to know and believe that if we are among those who try to do the right thing, God will not give us a test we cannot pass. Even if the situation SEEMS insurmountable, we just have to do what WE can to solve it, and trust in God for the rest.

The Jews who left Egypt with Moshe Rabbeinu did not do this. Instead, they allowed their own sense of unworthiness to intimidate them from even trying to confront the challenges that met them along their way. They focused on what they COULDN'T do for themselves, and assumed that God would not help them. Thus they were convinced that they were doomed to fail.

That was their first error, assuming that God would set them up to fail.

> Their second mistake was with respect to the concept of bitachon. In truth, nothing stands in the way of bitachon, as it says in the Midrash: "'One who trusts in God will be surrounded by kindness' (Tehillim 32:10); even an evil person who trusts in God will be surrounded by kindness" (Midrash Tehillim 32: 10). It further says there: "'Many are the agonies of the wicked' (Tehillim 32:10)—because he does not place his trust in the Holy One, blessed is He, and one who trusts in God, even an evil person, etc." (Midrash Tehillim 32:10). See there.

This is interesting. It is understandable that a "good" person, if he or she trusts in God, receives good. But an evil person? By trusting in God he can be more successful at...what? Stealing? Or whatever else he does to break the law? The merit of trusting in God can override the demerit of others sins?

According to the Midrash, apparently yes.

The Ramban says something similar in his work, HaEmunah v'HaBitachon, Ch. 1: "This is why it says, 'Trust in God and do good' (Tehillim 37:3), and does not say, 'Do good and trust in God.' Because trust in God does not depend on good deeds at all. Rather trust in God: whether you are righteous or evil, you should trust in God."

This is saying something rather AMAZING, and certainly something VERY encouraging. It is telling us that if a person happens to find himself in a situation that he cannot get out of without some kind of miracle, and believes that his many sins make him unworthy of one, he can STILL receive it—if he sincerely TRUSTS in God for it to happen. The trust alone will be the merit to make it happen.

Let's say, for example, someone needs to pay a large bill but doesn't have the money to do so. After considering every possible source of additional income, he still comes up short, and currently stands to lose his house to the bank if he doesn't find the funds soon.

So he prays to God for a miracle. As he does, he hears a little voice inside, saying, "How can you expect God to save you miraculously, when you have so many sins to your name? You do this, and you've done that, and you were about to do something else, etc. Just hearing your request for help after all the wrong you've done, the angels are probably rolling in the aisles with laughter!"

If he listens to that voice and gives up on himself and a miracle, then chances are he will have created a self-fulfilling prophecy. BUT if he thinks instead:

> "YES, I have a list of sins to fix up. But right now I need divine help. So for the time being I'm going to ignore the reasons God SHOULDN'T help me, and assume that God will also ignore them if I completely trust in Him right now. I'm going to try to believe with ALL my heart that He WILL come through for me."

According to Principle #2, God WILL save the day for him. God will in effect say:

> "Hmm, you have not been the most perfect person, and for that reason alone I should let you solve your problems for yourself. But... since you are willing to rely COMPLETELY on Me for your salvation, I'm going to provide it. I made this world for man to build a relationship with Me and to trust in Me completely.

When you sin, you clearly do not trust. But at this moment of crisis, you definitely do. That's enough for Me to help you out."

We learn how righteousness in the present can override sins of the past, and even of the future, from one of the last people we might think would teach it: Yishmael.[1] He had been sent into the desert[2] by Avraham Avinu and had become deathly ill along the way. Despite the evil he had been guilty of, and WOULD be guilty of in the future, God MIRACULOUSLY saved Yishmael's life because at THAT very moment he was contrite of spirit.

The Ramban continues:

"[The verse] concludes, however, with 'do good,' because if you do not [do teshuvah for past sins], then [Heaven] will exact payment from you nevertheless. The Holy One, blessed is He, is very patient, and will find a time to take payment from you." (Sefer Emunah u'Bitachon, Ch. 1)

This is the second half of the message, and it

---

[1] Rosh Hashanah 16b.
[2] Bereishis 21:14.

is just as important as the first half. Bitachon is enough to counteract past sins, but it does not eliminate them. A person still has to do teshuvah for his sins, and the sooner the better. He could find himself miraculously saved from one crisis by his bitachon, and later made to suffer another crisis because of his sins.

(Perhaps the words of the Chovos HaLevovos are [meant] in this way. See there, but regarding bitachon itself, nothing stands before it.)

The Chovos HaLevovos was the one who said that bitachon only "works" for the righteous.[3] The Leshem is trying to remove the point of disagreement by saying that perhaps he also agrees that bitachon works for anyone who uses it. But a person must endeavor to be righteous to avoid punishment at a later date in spite of the bitachon he previously had.

Specifically with regard to the matter of the Dor HaMidbar—whose entire fear was of being compromised by the yetzer hara, which is only intellectual and not actual, God forbid, as will be further explained—they should not

---

[3] See the previous chapter.

have feared at all, because this is the entire work of a person in this world, to persevere despite the scheming of the yetzer hara, and not to "spy" after it. There is no greater denial of the yetzer hara than this, and this is the basis of all the reward for Torah and mitzvos.

Many times in life a person finds himself in an ACTUAL scary situation. The problem is real, like being confronted by a dangerous person, having an incurable illness, or just being unable to pay a major debt on time. In such situations it is hard to imagine the problem just PEACEFULLY going away, which is why the yetzer hara can generate so much fear and doubt in divine salvation.

A lot of times, however, people worry about only POTENTIALLY dangerous situations as if they are already occurring. Anticipation is good when it is constructive, but not when it undermines our trust in God. That is the yetzer hara—what we're here to fight against—and therefore our success is the greatest source of eternal reward.

They had a great merit for trusting in God, and that He would constantly perform miracles and wonders for them with the light of "Atika Kadisha," which is the revelation of the light of Arich Anpin.

The situation of the Jews who were miraculously redeemed from Egypt was unique. God had sent them the greatest prophet to have ever lived, bringing with him a promise of redemption.[4] They had the MERIT to witness the supernatural and systematic destruction of the mightiest nation on the earth at that time. They MERITED to fulfill the dream of leaving the closed borders of Egypt in their lifetime. If ANY people had great reason to trust in God and His wonders, it was THIS generation.

All they had to do was constantly strengthen [faith] in God.

Rather than move backwards in their faith in God, they should have continuously increased it. In Egypt, their bitachon couldn't help but grow stronger, since each plague was a greater revelation of God. By the time the Plague of the First-born occurred, the revelation of God had become so intense that the Jewish people temporarily lost their free will.[5]

---

[4] Drushei Olam HaTohu, Chelek 2, Drush 5, Anaf 4, Siman 6.
[5] Drushei Olam HaTohu, Chelek 2, Drush 5, Anaf 2, Sim. 4-5.

Reaching the desert and beginning their journey to Mt. Sinai should not have undone any of that bitachon. They should have instead built upon their previous experiences and used them to integrate faith and trust in God into their very being. Instead of waiting for the next miracle to happen to make them trust further, they should have used—as we too should now use—past miracles to concretize bitachon.

Therefore, when they asked, "Is God among us or not?" it was as a test, and [indicated] complaint.

There are different ways to ask a question, innocently and provocatively. No one has a problem with the first kind of question, because people sincerely and constructively just want to know missing information.

It's the second kind of question that is off-putting. It shows contempt and, in the case of those who asked the question, a lack of appreciation for what had already been done for them. It may have sounded like an innocent question, but God's reaction shows that it was otherwise. He can read our heart, and know our true intention. As a result of not knowing the second principle—that NOTHING stands in the way of bitachon—

the people with Moshe assumed that their past sins did stand in the way, and therefore we read:

> It was a sin and blemish for them, which is why the verse speaks disparagingly about them, saying, "Because they did not believe in God and did not trust in His salvation." It was because of their lack of trust, as mentioned. This is what it also says, "they...did not trust in His salvation," which means that they did not believe in themselves...

They thought that it was unlikely:

> ...that they were worthy of constant wonders. All this was a function of their minimal trust, as all that has been said will be further explained later, with the help of God.

A search for trust

six

Misplaced Righteousness

THE FEAR OF losing money is one of the "secrets" of how to keep it. The fear makes people more cautious and encourages them find ways to make even more money, while protecting what they already have. It makes them think before spending it.

The same thing is true of righteousness. If people fear sin, they will be more cautious not to commit one. They will learn both what constitutes a sin and what causes it to happen. This will eventually make them righteous.

This was the case with Dovid HaMelech, who

wrote, "My sin is always before me."[1] What he meant was that since he was aware of how easy it is to sin, he needed to be mindful of the opportunities that came up in order to avoid them. This made him pious.[2]

But it is one thing to fear sin, and something totally different to allow it to interfere with one's bitachon, as even some of the greatest people have done:

> If we contemplate this, we find more. In a similar manner, certain elevated holy people have stumbled in this somewhat. They are from those who are strong in the performing of His word, and whose entire hearts and souls are constantly directed to God, and they have stumbled in this manner, but not to test or complain, God forbid! but in contriteness and fear, because of their great holiness and humility. On their level, however, it was considered damaging and a blemish.

God judges us relative to our spiritual level. A sin for one person may not be a sin for another person, because of the difference in spiritual ca-

---

[1] Tehillim 51:3.
[2] Brochos 4a.

pacity. A person is held responsible only for what he COULD have done better, but didn't, something only God can accurately calculate.

This is why it is called stumbling "somewhat." When a righteous person lacks bitachon, it is only in comparison to the high level he usually lives with. And the reason for the lack often is a reflection of his general humility and his not wanting to rely on his spiritual greatness to guarantee himself a miraculous salvation.

Nevertheless, it is still considered a lack of bitachon for such a person, and it's wrong:

> This is as our rabbis say in Pesikta d'Rav Kahana, Piska "b'Chodesh HaShvi'i," and also in Vayikra Rabbah, Ch. 29, Siman 2: "'But as for you, do not fear, My servant Ya'akov, the word of God, and do not be afraid, Yisroel, etc.' (Yirmiyahu 30:10), because in the vision of the ladder, The Holy One, blessed is He, showed Ya'akov Avinu the angel of Bavel ascending and descending, of Medai ascending and descending, of Yavan ascending and descending, and of Edom ascending and descending. The Holy One, blessed is He, said to him, 'Ya'akov, you ascend as well.' At that time Ya'akov Avinu became afraid and said, 'Per-

haps, God forbid, just as these descended, so too will I descend!'"

The Torah's version of the dream of the ladder is very brief.[3] The Midrash elaborates and includes additional and VERY IMPORTANT details of the prophecy Ya'akov Avinu had that night as he dreamed of the ladder. The dream was not NEARLY as simple and straightforward as the Torah makes it seem.

According to the Midrash, after seeing all the angels representing the four exiles the Jewish people were destined to endure over thousands of years until the Final Redemption, Ya'akov was told to ascend as well. Assuming that ascending the ladder meant ascendancy and descending it meant downfall, Ya'akov balked. Understandably, he didn't want to share the same fate as those who would later exile his descendants.

"The Holy One, blessed is He, said to him, 'Do not be afraid, my servant Ya'akov. If you ascend, you will never descend.'"

This was the game changer. Until that moment, God had not minded Ya'akov's hesitation.

---

[3] Bereishis 28:12.

On the contrary, God told Ya'akov that his fate would be different from that of the angels if he would just trust and ascend the ladder. With such divine assurance, apparently, Ya'akov Avinu should have been able to push all concern aside and climb with confidence.

Instead:

> "He did not believe Him and did not ascend. Rebi Berachya…elucidated, in the name of Rebi Meir, '"Nevertheless, they sinned further and had no faith in His wonders" (Tehillim 78:32). This is Ya'akov Avinu, who did not believe and did not ascend.'"

This verse, as mentioned earlier, refers to the Jews of Moshe Rabbeinu's time. However, Rebi Berachya says that it also applies to Ya'akov Avinu, who, according to the Midrash, erred similarly with respect to bitachon—and we have been paying the price ever since:

> "The Holy One, Blessed is He, said to him, 'Had you believed in Me and ascended, you would never have descended. Since you did not believe in Me and ascend, your children are destined to undergo four exiles in this world…'"

Although it was only a dream, it was also a prophecy, and had historic consequences. The Midrash speaks of the four exiles alluded to in the second verse of the Creation story.[4] Later, Ya'akov's dream reiterated the prophecy, with the angels ascending and descending the ladder. The four exiles seem to have been part and parcel of Jewish history.

But actually not! Apparently Ya'akov could have prevented all four exiles before any of them even began, just by climbing the ladder...in his dream! The Midrash concludes:

> "At that time Ya'akov feared and said to the Holy One, blessed is He, 'Master of the universe, forever?'"

When Ya'akov heard the news, he feared that he had doomed his descendants to eternal exile and suffering:

> "He answered him, 'Do not be afraid, Yisroel, for behold, I am saving you from afar' (Yirmiyahu 30:10), etc. (Vayikra Rabbah 29:2)." See there. When they say that Ya'akov Avinu, a"h, did not believe in His wonders, they mean in

---

4 Bereishis Rabbah 2:4.

the same manner that it was said regarding the Dor HaMidbar, that he did not believe himself worthy of the Holy One, blessed be He, doing wonders for him.

When it came to the Dor HaMidbar, they had sufficient reason to doubt themselves. They had just been slaves, heavily involved in idol worship, and had yet to receive Torah. It was hard for them to fathom how such unworthy people could enjoy such special Divine Providence.

Ya'akov Avinu, however, did nothing BUT serve God. If anyone was worthy of a supernatural existence, he was. But his humility made him doubt his own worthiness, and although humility is normally admirable, here it worked against him.

Furthermore, for Ya'akov Avinu all this was in a prophetic vision in a dream, in a vision of the ladder. All this was the level of a prophetic vision, as per the verse, "In a dream I will speak to him" (Bamidbar 12:6). Nevertheless, it proceeded like a dream.

Another important distinction between Ya'akov Avinu and the Generation of the Desert is that his "sin" occurred in a dream, not in reality as it had done for the Dor HaMidbar. How does an unconscious person make a choice for which he and all of his descendants can later be held responsible?

> See the Zohar, Parashas Vayaitzai 149a in "Sisrei Torah," and Parashas Mishpatim 119a. They also say in Midrash Tehillim 78 regarding the dream of Ya'akov Avinu, a"h, "There is no dream without an interpretation." See there.

This is the answer to the question. Dreams and prophecies may occur when we are unconscious, but they allude to conscious realities. Like Yosef's dreams, they are subject to interpretations that can and often do play out in some form or other in everyday life.

Ya'akov Avinu's fear and refusal to ascend the ladder in his dream was indicative of his approach to his life. It was a part of him, and it would eventually dictate a similar reaction in a real-life circumstance for which he COULD be held accountable.

> This is our matter. The Holy One, blessed is He, also told him, "I am with you and I will protect you, etc." (Bereishis 28:16). After that, He told him moreover in Parashas Vayaitzai

(31:3), "Return to the land of your fathers…
and I will be with you." Nevertheless, when he
came to Eisav, he was afraid of him, as will be
explained.

On more than one occasion God assured
Ya'akov Avinu that he would be protected. Once
that was the case, it was no longer an issue of
feeling unworthy of supernatural protection, because God had promised it! This was similar to
God telling Ya'akov in his dream that if he climbed
the ladder, he would never descend.

Yet when Ya'akov confronted Eisav on his
way home from Lavan, he did so in fear, as if he
didn't really believe that God would protect him.
That was similar to his refusing to climb the ladder in the dream, and for this reaction to Eisav he
was ultimately held accountable, making the four
exiles inevitable for his descendants.

Regarding this, they said that he did not believe in His wonders, as mentioned. This is
the interpretation of the dream mentioned,
as will later be explained at length.

In conclusion, there is a time and place for
just about everything. Humility is one of the most
important traits for a person to develop and live

by, but not to the point that it interferes with a person's trust in God. Whether righteous or evil, a person has to believe in God and His wonders, and leave the rest to Him.

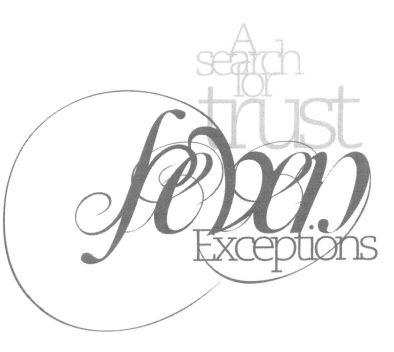

A search for trust

fear.

Exceptions

FEAR IS A very powerful emotion, and a dangerous one as well. It can be a motivator for great good, or a reason for terrible bad. It does not only cause us to perceive threat where it doesn't exist, but also makes us react as if it actually did exist. Ironically, many people tend to fear what they shouldn't, rather than what they should.

This is the matter. As it is known, a fear of sin is a trait and level of which there is none higher, as it says: "Fortunate is the person who constantly fears" (Mishlei 28:14).

The goal is to be righteous. This means doing as many mitzvos and avoiding as many sins as possible. It would be easy if it weren't for the yetzer hara and subjugation to foreign powers, as the Talmud states:

> Rav Alexandri on concluding his prayer used to add the following: "Master of the universe, You know well that our will is to perform Your will. And what prevents us? The 'yeast in the dough,' and subjection to the foreign powers." (Brochos 17a)

The "yeast in the dough" refers to the yetzer hara, since man was "kneaded" from the ground. It is called "yeast" because the yetzer hara tends to bloat a person's ego, and discourage the performance of mitzvos while encouraging sin.

It hasn't helped that the Jewish people have been subjugated by foreign powers either. They have often made it next to impossible to properly perform mitzvos, while making it much easier to do just the opposite.

Thus the verse says, "Fortunate is the person who constantly fears" passing up opportunities to perform mitzvos, and also fears committing sins. This is the only real protection a person has against the yetzer hara. Thus the Torah writes:

Now, Israel, what does God, your God, ask of you? Only to fear God, your God, etc." (Devarim 10:12)

The Talmud states:

All is in the hands of Heaven except the fear of God. (Brochos 33b)

Rabbah bar Rav Huna said: "Anyone who possesses learning without the fear of Heaven is like a treasurer who is entrusted with the inner keys but not with the outer. How is he to enter?"

Rebi Yannai proclaimed: "Woe to the person who has no courtyard, yet makes a gate for one!"

Rav Yehudah said: "The Holy One, blessed is He, created His world only so that men should fear Him, etc." (Shabbos 31b)

Thus a fear of God, which is a really a fear of sin, is essential for staying on the straight and narrow. But as the Leshem points out:

The main point, however, is to protect a person from coming to sin. To fear that maybe "a sin will cause" is not a trait of the righteous at all…

Clearly they are two different types of fear. One is a fear of committing sins, which leaves a person on guard against them. The other is a fear that sins will turn God against the person, and make him unworthy of divine help. And not just fear of past sins, but even of sins yet to be committed. There is nothing righteous about this, the Leshem continues:

> …as it is written: "Of evil tidings he will have no fear. His heart is firm, confident in God" (Tehillim 112:7). Since his "heart is firm, confident in God," "his heart is steadfast; he shall not fear" (Tehillim 112:8). It is as the commentators explain there, and mentioned earlier in Siman 3 regarding bitachon…

The key words here are "confident in God," NO MATTER WHAT. There's just no reason NOT to trust completely in God…

> Especially someone who does not feel he has any sins, and even more so someone who has a PROMISE from the Holy One, blessed is He.

> If a person KNOWS he has sinned, and yet is

told that he still must trust in God for success, then how much more so a person who believes he has NOT sinned, and even more so if he has been promised by God to be protected, as Ya'akov Avinu was.

Yes, sin occurs. Yes, it can make a person worthy of punishment, and therefore necessitate teshuvah. But that is a different matter altogether. In the meantime, a person must strengthen his or her trust in God, especially during a time of crisis.

> There is no need to ask about many earlier holier people who had to suffer many pains and evils, why they did not make use of the trait of bitachon and then certainly be saved.

The Leshem has anticipated a very important question, crucial for a person accepting the two principles of bitachon and emunah, especially the second one. If nothing stands in the way of bitachon, why has it not worked in the past for people who clearly had it, like the great Rebi Akiva, whose death is recounted in the Talmud?

> When Rebi Akiva was taken out for execution, it was the time to say the "Shema." While they combed his flesh with iron combs, he accepted upon himself the king-

ship of Heaven. His students said to him: "Our teacher! Even to this point?"

He answered them: "All my life I have been troubled by this verse [from the Shema, 'You shall serve God...] with all your soul' [which I interpret to mean] that even if He takes your soul. I asked, 'When will I have the opportunity to fulfill this?' Now that I have the opportunity, should I not fulfill it?"

He prolonged the word "echad," and died while saying it." (Brochos 61b)

In fact, every Yom Kippur and Tisha b'Av we recount how the Romans brutally killed 10 of the greatest rabbis to have ever lived. Why didn't bitachon, which clearly they had plenty of, not save THEM from death? If it didn't work for them, how is it supposed to work for lesser people?

What about thousands of years of pogroms, the largest and most recent of all being the Holocaust which murdered SIX MILLION Jews? Without doubt the numbers have included extremely righteous people, who died "prematurely" at the hands of their enemies with their bitachon STILL intact. Something certainly stood in the way of bitachon in all these cases!

You should know, however, that they had a

different trait. They accepted their suffering with love, as it says regarding Rebi Akiva, Brochos 61a, "All my life I have been troubled, etc. 'When will I have the opportunity to fulfill this?'"

In other words, when he was arrested for breaking Roman law and teaching Torah in public Rebi Akiva was not captured and tortured by the Romans because he had no alternative. Because of his bitachon, he COULD have MIRACULOUSLY survived his situation if he had chosen to, as Rebi Shimon Bar Yochai had done when he hid in a cave for 13 years.

But Rebi Akiva didn't choose to survive. Instead, as he told his students in his final moments, he had LONGED for the opportunity to fulfill the words of the "Shema," to die for the sake of God and Torah. He had taught Torah against Roman decree to keep it alive. But after he was captured for doing so, Rebi Akiva had embraced the opportunity and LOVINGLY died "al Kiddush Hashem," sanctifying the name of God.

It was similar with respect to Rebi Elazar b'Rebi Shimon in Bava Metzia 84b: "Come, my brothers and dear ones, etc."

The Talmud recounts how Rebi Elazar b'Rebi Shimon had brought upon himself suffering for the sake of teshuvah. Yet despite his extreme pain, he allowed the rabbis of his time to come to his home and learn with him. Why hadn't he simply used his bitachon to save himself from all HIS suffering?

> They did not want to bother their Maker, and rather made use of the trait of "Mesiras Nefesh," that is, they sacrificed themselves to the Holy One, blessed is He, may His name be blessed, to do with them as He saw fit. They specifically did not want to trouble their Maker to do their will.

Mesiras Nefesh, or self-sacrifice, is incumbent upon every Jew when it comes to the service of God. It's the only real way to measure one's devotion to God and Torah, and earn reward in Olam HaBa—the World-to-Come. Mesiras Nefesh is, in effect, the "currency" of the next, eternal world.

In everyday life, it is really up to individuals to determine how much of themselves they are willing to put into their mitzvos. There is a minimum, as set out in the Shulchan Aruch, the complete body of Jewish law, and its many commentaries. But beyond that minimum, it is really up to us to decide how much the mitzvah means to us, and how much eternal reward we want to earn.

Sometimes, in certain situations, a Jew has to be willing to die to sanctify the name of God. Many have done so over the ages, even when they could have lived by doing what their captors demanded instead of what the Torah commands. They loved God and Torah more than a life that profaned both.

However, there have been times when death could have been avoided without profaning the name of God. For example, a miracle could have been invoked, as was common in Rebi Akiva's time, to avoid death. The following example is in the Talmud. Rebi Yannai said:

> Tefillin demand a pure body, like Elisha "Ba'al Kanafyim"…And why is he called "Ba'al Kanafyim"? Because the evil state once proclaimed a decree against the Jewish people that whoever wore tefillin would have his brains pierced. Still, Elisha put them on and went out into the streets. A soldier saw him and he fled before him, while the latter chased after him. As he overtook him, he [Elisha] removed them from his head and held them in his hand. "What is that in your hand?" he demanded.

"The wings of a dove," he answered.

He opened his hand and the wings of a dove were in it. Therefore he is called Elisha "Ba'al Kanafyim." (Shabbos 130a)

The Talmud is filled with many examples of life-saving miracles from the time of the Tannaim. In fact, in the account of the death of the Ten Martyrs included in the Chazan's repetition of the Mussaf on Yom Kippur, there is an interesting but often overlooked detail.

After being told by the Caesar that they were to die as atonement for Yosef's brothers, the 10 rabbis destined to become the "Ten Martyrs" asked for three days to consider the matter, and what was just as strange, the Roman leader granted it.

What was supposed to happen at the end of those three days? Were they going to come back to the Caesar and say, "We discussed the matter among ourselves and decided, no, we're not going to die"? Was the Caesar going to answer, "Oh, okay, then go on your way, and don't forget to live long and fulfilling lives"?

As we read, Rebi Yishmael used the time to go into a state of prophecy, and learn from Heaven itself what was to be his fate, and the fate of his colleagues. It was Gavriel who told him that all of them were to die al Kiddush Hashem because, as

Kabbalah explains, the world needed this in order to survive.

And if not? If their deaths were NOT necessary for human existence, how would they have changed their situation and ended their predicament in their favor? The same way they had done so many other times before, with Kabbalah. They were the ultimate miracle workers, and did all kinds of fantastic things at will. Had the world not required something greater than their miracles to survive, they could have bested the Caesar at his own game.

This is why they asked the Caesar for the three days to consider the matter. The halachah states that if someone does not have to die al Kiddush Hashem, but does so anyhow, he is guilty of and punishable for taking his own life. Before making the supreme sacrifice for God, it's necessary to make sure that's what it actually is.

Once the rabbis confirmed that it really was necessary, these historically great individuals submitted to the will of the Caesar. And much to his chagrin, they used the opportunity to rectify the world the Romans were destroying, by turning themselves into spectacles of devotion to God and Torah. In one instance, a Roman executioner was so impressed that he regretted his role in the death of a rabbi, and converted on the spot.

So yes, NOTHING stands in the way of bitachon—when a person truly has it—except the higher purpose of sanctifying the name of God. The fact that great believers have died in spite of their bitachon only means that they chose that higher purpose over life itself, and an eternal bond with God that supersedes any kind of continued existence in this world.

There is another exception, however, as the Leshem explains:

> There is also another hidden matter. Sometimes it is His will, may His name be blessed, to specifically bring a decree, along the lines of "Kavshei d'Rachmana," of His hidden thoughts, may His name be blessed. Then He will remove free will and put fear in their hearts, until it is impossible to be strong in the trait of bitachon, in order to fulfill the decree in any case, may God have mercy upon us.

The last 2,000 years of Jewish history have not been easy. Only in recent times have Jews enjoyed such peace and equality, at least compared to earlier times, the only real exception being the "Golden Era" in Spain from about 912–1031 CE. The rest of the time the Jewish people were treated as second-class citizens at best, and ruthlessly slaughtered at worst.

Antisemitism originally could have been considered religious racism. In the beginning, just about every culture was religious, and had zero tolerance for those who did not go along with their program. The Jewish people, who were often the most obstinate, usually chose death over conversion.

But although religion has waned in the Western world, antisemitism has not. The Holocaust was not perpetrated by the Church but rather by a completely secular culture that prided itself on its advance intellectualism. Jews were hunted, captured, and murdered only because they were Jewish, even after successfully doing everything they could to be like their gentile hosts.

It is because, contrary to conventional wisdom, antisemitism is NOT simply racism. It is obviously similar in many external ways, but at its deadly heart, it is something very different. It is a different track of Hashgochah Pratis—Divine Providence—of its own.

The Torah speaks about this in both Parashas Bechukosai and Ki Savo. Known as the "curses," the long list of reactions of the Divine to Jewish disobedience is less about punishment and more about tikun, or compensation. The Jewish people were given Torah as a means to partner with God in the perfection of Creation. If this doesn't happen BECAUSE of them, then it will happen THROUGH them, as it has been doing in the form of all kinds of national suffering.

Sometimes, specifically during the time of prophecy, the Jewish people had a way to find out in advance if they were heading towards bad times. This allowed them to internally make national tikunim before God imposed bad things from the outside via attacking nations or natural disasters.

Prophecy, however, came to an end after the Purim Miracle, and even before it did, people had become too brazen to listen to it anyhow. Without prophecy, the means to know what God was intending in advance of disaster was gone, and more often than not, disaster came regardless. The rest is history, an often bloody history.

Those are the decrees the Leshem is talking about. Only God knows what Creation needs, and what has to be done to provide it. Sometimes tikun may not even involve the Jewish people, at least directly, while at other times it specifically affects the Jewish people.

There is a line in the sand. Once history passes it, and Torah and mitzvos become incapable of providing the necessary tikun in time, then events that MUST happen are set in motion. They are the events of history that CANNOT and WILL NOT be stopped—for the future good of mankind.

Consequently, God takes drastic steps to make sure that this is the case. We know from Moshe Rabbeinu that, when necessary for the sake of history, God interferes with man's free will. On several occasions, God "hardened" Pharaoh's heart so that he would not let the Jewish people go. By being obstinate when he could have CHOSEN to do the right thing, Pharaoh lost the choice to do right, and he could no long choose NOT to do the bad thing.

It is hard to comprehend how a single righteous person, or even a few, can mitigate the judgment of billions of people, but they can. That's how powerful free will and devotion to God are. The deaths of the Ten Martyrs didn't only save an entire generation—it saved many following generations as well.

Therefore, if God wants to carry out a "gazerah" against a particular generation, He has to first "neutralize" the merit of the righteous people living in it. He does this by suspending their free will to trust in Him, making them unnaturally vulnerable to fears without which they would have trusted in God to protect them and their generation.

Is that fair? It has to be, even if we can't see how. One thing is for certain: the tzaddik will be rewarded for the bitachon he WOULD have had, in any case. He will be rewarded in Olam HaBa for the generation he WOULD have saved, had his free will been left alone. It is the generation itself that loses out when the need to fulfill a divine decree necessitates such an extreme measure.

> This is similar to what the great Rebi Ya'akov of Lisa said in the name of the Ramban in his elucidation of Megillas Esther, on the verse, "And Mordechai would not bend or bow" (Esther 3:2). See there. But in truth, nothing stands in the way of bitachon, and with respect to this it says, "But the righteous are as confident as a young lion" (Mishlei 28:1).

The Leshem concludes that when it comes to the rest of history, nothing stands in the way of bitachon, whether a person is righteous or evil. And for the record, even during times of "Shmad," when the enemies of the Jewish people have free reign to do as they please to the nation, bitachon can still save the day for individuals or even entire groups.

There are many stories of this throughout

Jewish history. Even during the Holocaust miracles occurred for individuals whose trust in God did not waver, not even during the most dire moments. The following is but one such account from a person who one day gave a lift to a survivor of World War II.

I once gave a lift to an older man who had survived the Holocaust many decades earlier. We got to talking, and eventually he told me a story that just amazed me. He said that as a young man during the war, he was spotted by a couple of Nazi soldiers, who chased after him and commanded him to stop. He of course just kept running away, until he found himself in a dead-end alley. He didn't know what to do as he desperately looked for a place to hide, knowing that his capture and death were imminent. Just before the soldiers turned the corner, he noticed an electrical box big enough for him to climb into and hide. But, he realized, the two soldiers would also see the box and discover his hiding place. As he heard them coming closer, he tried to think of something to pray to protect himself, but all he could think of was the following verse: "They struck the men who were at the entrance of the house with blindness" (Bereishis 19:11). This is the verse about the angels who blinded the people of Sdom who wanted to molest them, saving Lot and his family from danger. So he said the verse to himself over and over again, as he heard the soldiers coming closer and closer. Sure enough, they discovered the electrical box and were opening it while he continued to say the verse to himself. With the box open, the soldiers looked inside. Seeing "nothing," they closed the box and went on their way. Shocked and eternally grateful for what was nothing short of a GREAT miracle, the boy eventually made his way to freedom and survived to tell his story many decades later.

This is just one of many, but still far too few, stories of miraculous escapes from relentless and vicious enemies. There are very many others we don't even know about, and will only find out about later in the World-to-Come.

NOTHING stands in the way of BITACHON.

A search for trust

eight

Promise for Sin

IT IS IRONIC that the people who don't worry about sinning are the ones who most need to worry about it and about how it might disrupt their relationship with God. The ones who don't need to worry, the righteous, are the ones who do worry, but sometimes for the wrong reason:

> Returning to the matter, removing bitachon out of a fear of sin is not a righteous trait.

Fear of sin is real. It makes people anticipate the potential for sin and avoid it, encouraging righteousness. But there is NO purpose at all for the fear that a sin will occur in the future to make a person unworthy of God's help, thus making bitachon irrelevant. Bitachon works for anyone who uses it, righteous or not.

> Our rabbis say in Bereishis Rabbah, Ch. 76, Siman 1, that the Jewish people deserved to be wiped out in the days of Haman (because they feared so much and did not trust in God; see there and Pesikta Rabba, Piska 33). If only they had not relied on the thinking of "the Elder," their father! They said, "Just as our father Ya'akov feared, whom the Holy One, blessed is He, promised, 'I am with you,' how much more so should we!"

This point is not clear from Megillas Esther. The story begins with the 180-day drinking feast of King Achashveros and recounts how, while drunk, he had his wife, Vashti, executed. The Jewish people and how they lived at that time are not mentioned at that point in the Megillah itself.

The story then turns to Haman's rise in power to second-in-command over Persia. As a result, we are also introduced to Mordechai, since he is the one who will instigate Haman and "inspire" him to make a decree against the Jewish people, who at that time seemed to be minding their own business. From the Megillah it seems as if Mordechai single-handedly endangered his entire nation!

It is the Talmud and Midrash that provide more accurate glimpses of what was really happening then. Yes, it was Mordechai who earned the wrath of Haman, but it was the Jewish people THEMSELVES who had earned the wrath of God, making them worthy of DIVINE destruction via Haman's decree.

Why? Because they feared Haman too much, rather than trusting in God. Although Mordechai had not feared Haman, and had insisted that the rest of the nation follow suit, they said, "If Ya'akov Avinu was unsure about HIS future despite God's promise to protect him, how much more so should WE worry about not receiving divine protection from OUR enemy."

Wrong! Ya'akov was wrong in his time, and they were even more wrong in theirs:

> This is what the prophet bothered the Jewish people about, and said to them, "Who are you that you fear man, who will die...And you forgot God, your Maker..." (Yeshayahu 51:12-13). See there and Pesikta Rabbah.

From the Megillah it seems as if the Jewish people of Haman's time had good reason to fear. Haman was an Amaleki, an existential enemy, on the warpath to kill every last Jew. According to the prophet Yeshayahu, however, they wouldn't have had to fear if they had just trusted in God. Ironically, their very fear of Haman was what made him into someone to be feared.

This is an important point about bitachon. A lack of trust in God can actually lead to the occurrence of the very problem that the person worried about. "If I trust in God," the person worries, "and He doesn't come through, I'll be in trouble." In response to that, God says, "Let's see if you can succeed when you DON'T trust in Me!"

Thus, contrary to what some people believe, or at least emotionally feel, the odds of salvation greatly decrease when they STOP trusting in God. They may be able to RELATE better to a means they can see, but they have a perfect chance of succeeding with God, the "means" they CAN'T see.

Although this may not always be apparent in the SHORT run, it definitely is in the LONG run. Success and failure can involve many steps. What seems like success can over time end up being just the opposite, and vice-versa. There are many stories of people who thought their trust in God failed them, only to find out later that just the opposite was true.

> Also with respect to Ya'akov Avinu, a"h, he was afraid that maybe "a sin would cause," as it says in Brochos 4a. Nevertheless, our rabbis take him to task for this, and say in Bereishis Rabbah, Ch. 75, Siman 3: When Ya'akov sent messengers and gifts, it was like grabbing the ear of a dog, causing it to bite him.

After being away from home for 34 years, first for 14 years in the yeshivah of Shem and Eiver, and then for 20 years with Lavan, his father-in-law, Ya'akov decided it was time to come home. And THAT, it seems from the Torah, meant once again confronting his vengeful brother, Eisav, whom he had avoided by leaving home in the first place. From the Torah, it seems that their confrontation was inevitable.

When Ya'akov Avinu was close enough, he sent messengers and gifts to Eisav to try to placate him. And when Eisav finally came out to meet Ya'akov, Ya'akov bowed down to him seven times, eventually further humbling himself to Eisav by calling himself Eisav's "servant."

Ya'akov's strategy seemed to work, because Eisav's mercy was aroused. What could have easily been a deadly fight to the finish turned out peacefully instead. Afterwards, they bid each other farewell and went in opposite directions—forever.

Everything seemed to go well for Ya'akov Avinu and his entourage, and had it not been for the Midrash's take on what happened, we'd never have known otherwise. It is the Midrash that tells us about how the entire confrontation was unnecessarily dangerous, and resulted in who knows how much death and destruction from Eisav's descendants!

Apparently the confrontation between Ya'akov and Eisav had NOT been inevitable. In fact, Chazal compare it to walking up to a dog that was minding its own business, pulling its ear and thus causing it to bite. Had Eisav fought Ya'akov instead of making peace, Ya'akov's "wound" would have been considered self-inflicted![1]

---

[1] He went out of his way to draw Eisav out because he deemed the confrontation necessary as part of the all-important and historic process of transforming himself from "Ya'akov" to "Yisroel." Given that the night before the confrontation he had fought the angel of Eisav, won, and had his name changed from "Ya'akov" to "Yisroel," he must have been on the right track. Chazal may not be faulting him as much as pointing out that Ya'akov chose the risk on his own, since God would not have commanded him to risk his life like that. It had to be a personal act of self-sacrifice.

The Holy One, Blessed is He, said to him, "He was going on his way, and you sent to him and said to him, 'So says your servant Ya'akov.'" This is what the verse says in Yirmiyahu 13:21, "What will you say when He punishes you? You yourself have trained them as rulers over you…" (Yirmiyahu 13:21).

Furthermore, although Ya'akov's and Eisav's meeting did end on a good note between the two of them, that wasn't the case with God. It was one thing for Ya'akov to be gracious, but it was something altogether different to completely demean himself before his murderous brother:

> It says in Pirkei d'Rebi Eliezer, at the end of Ch. 37, that when Ya'akov Avinu, a"h, said, "So says your servant Ya'akov" (Bereishis 32:4), "the Holy One, blessed is He, said to him, 'It is not enough that you profaned your holy self, but I said, "The elder will serve the younger one" (Bereishis 25:23), and you said, "your servant Ya'akov"! By your life, as you said! He will rule over you in this world,'" and you will rule over him in the World-to-Come.

The Midrash says that Ya'akov told God that he acted as he did with Eisav in order to save his life. As a result, we learn from this that it is permissible to flatter dangerous enemies to avoid trouble. Yet God was not happy with Ya'akov, because his actions both debased him and also went against the prophecy given at the time of Ya'akov's birth.

The consequences of Ya'akov Avinu's "mistake" have been both devastating and far reaching. An hour of error, according to the Midrash, has translated into THOUSANDS of years of the worst kind of subjugation to Eisav's descendants. That's how much tikun it has taken to make right by the "end" of Jewish history what went wrong at the "beginning" of it. We may "own" the World-to-Come, but it is Eisav who has clearly "owned" this world.

> Likewise, the commentators ask further regarding the matter of what "maybe a sin will cause," from the Yerushalmi, Sanhedrin, Ch. 11, Halachah 5, and likewise the Midrash Tanchuma, Parashas Vayaira, Siman 13. It is brought in the Rambam, in Hilchos Yesodei HaTorah, Ch. 10, Halachah 4, that all good that has come from the mouth of the Holy One, blessed is He, is never rescinded, even because of sin. See the Tanchuma there, and also the gemora Brochos 7a, at the end of

Side A, as well as Shabbos 55a.

It turns out that there is an additional problem with the idea of worrying about how possible sins can undermine future heavenly help, negating the need for bitachon. It has to do with a principle of Divine Providence that says that positive prophecies MUST come true. If God says that something good will happen in the future, it WILL, no matter WHAT.

The source of this is a prophecy from Yirmiyahu 28:7-8); see Rashi there.

The Leshem does not quote the verse from Yirmiyahu, but Rashi does:

Listen now to this thing that I speak in your ears and in the ears of all the people. (Yirmiyahu 28:7)

He said, "I prophesy retribution, but if it does not come, I am not a liar, since the Holy One, blessed be He, renounces the evil. But the prophet who prophesies for peace...if his word does not come, he is a liar... (Rashi)

Seemingly the verse, as Rashi explains, says

that a prophecy for bad does not have to come true. A prophecy for good, however, does. On the other hand:

> In truth, in Yirmiyahu itself, Ch. 18, it says: "One moment I may speak concerning a nation or a kingdom, to destroy, demolish, or annihilate [it], but if that nation repents of its evil deed of which I had spoken...Or one moment I may speak concerning a nation or a kingdom, to build and establish [it], but if they do what is wrong in My eyes, not heeding My voice, then I relent of the good that I had said to bestow upon it." It explains there that a promise for good can change because of a sin.

But these verses, earlier said by the same prophet, say just the opposite—that a good prophecy CAN be overturned because of sin. It's an obvious contradiction.

> See the Maharsha on this in Chiddushei Aggados, Brochos, p. 4. He brings there in the name of the Ba'al Akeidah, Sha'ar 96, and Mizrachi, Parashas Vayishlach. See the Lechem Mishnah on the Rambam, Yesodei Ha-Torah, at the end of Ch. 10. However, it seems

to me that the main idea is that a prophecy of good does not change, even because of sin, as the Midrash Tanchuma explains in Parashas Vayaira, Siman 13; see there. However, what it says in Yirmiyahu, Ch. 18, verse 10, that good can also change because of sin, means when the sin is because of the promise itself. They rely upon the promise and are lenient on themselves to pursue the desires of their heart, certain about the good. The promise becomes the reason for the sin for them, and for this the promise of good can change.

Of the many great abilities of the Leshem, one of his greatest is the way he is able to resolve apparent conflicts within Torah elegantly and insightfully. His answer to the contradictory verses from Yirmiyahu is another case in point.

The Leshem suggests that the difference in the two situations is the basis of the sins. If the sins are the result of spiritual weaknesses, or just spiritual insensitivities, then it will NOT change God's mind about any good He may have previously promised the Jewish people. He can always punish the nation for sins lacking teshuvah, but the good promised will still happen.

But, says the Leshem, if the brazenness to sin

is the promise of good itself, then God will overturn it. Nothing is more offensive than using the good received against the one who gave it, especially when it was promised to promote just the opposite behavior.

Therefore if a person thinks, "I can afford to sin because God has promised us good, and all that God says for good MUST come true," God answers, "Except in this case. I never promised any good that is the basis of sin. 'Then I relent of the good that I had said to bestow upon it.'"

Now it makes sense why good still comes to people who don't seem to merit it on their own. There have been many times in Jewish history when sinners have prospered.

It is one thing for God to be patient with sinners, not punishing them while waiting for them to do teshuvah. It is far more difficult, however, to reconcile their apparent prosperity in the meantime, before they have even gotten around to doing teshuvah, if they ever will.[2]

---

[2] The modern State of Israel is a good case in point. The country was settled and is "protected" by many Jews who do not keep the most basic Torah laws. Yet the country has MIRACULOUSLY thrived and repelled all its many enemies over the last seven decades, fulfilling many ancient prophecies! Perhaps it is because they don't rely on God's promises of good to sin, allowing the good to still occur for the nation as a whole, including those who do not live by Torah.

Not, according to the Leshem, if the good was promised independent of the sinners, and they are not relying upon the promise to sin. The good will still happen, and so will their punishment if they do not do teshuvah in time. That is when nothing stands in the way of bitachon.

> This is similar to what it says in Yoma 85b: "A person who says, 'I will sin and Yom Kippur will atone for me,' Yom Kippur will not atone."

This is called, "sinning on the condition to repent," and it's a serious miscalculation:

> The reason is because he makes Yom Kippur the reason for the sin, and it is similar in our matter, as mentioned.

Yes, Yom Kippur is a day of atonement, but only as long as the day itself doesn't become an excuse for sin. Yom Kippur was given to the Jewish people as a gift, to allow us to rectify sins that were regretfully committed, not for sins that were committed for the sake of Yom Kippur.

> It was also the same with respect to Ya'akov Avinu, a"h, regarding "maybe a sin will cause." What he meant was that he was un-

certain of himself, concerned lest the promise cause him to be lenient with himself, which would make the promise the reason for the sin, God forbid. As a consequence, the promise would not be fulfilled at all.

This means that Ya'akov Avinu did not just worry about future sins overturning God's promises of future good. He worried that the promises themselves would make him overconfident, perhaps even spiritually lax. It is the nature of human beings—one that must be counteracted—to take good for granted.

If such an attitude leads to sin, then could it not be counted as a promise being the basis of sin? If yes, would such sin not be a reason to overturn the promise for good itself? Perhaps, the Leshem explains, this was Ya'akov Avinu's deeper concern. It says...

Similarly in Bereishis Rabbah Ch. 76, Siman 2: "There is no promise for the righteous in this world." But other than this, a promise for good does not change because of any sin.

In other words, the Midrash is saying that righteous people, such as Ya'akov Avinu, tend not to want to rely on promises for good. This means, as the Leshem explains, that they can't indulge in lenient behavior that could, God forbid, result in sin.

A search for trust

אין

No Sacrifice
At All

IT'S LIKE BORROWING a hammer, deliberately using it to break the lender's window, and then expecting to be forgiven for the damage. How self-serving and offensive can one get? But that is what it is like for God when someone uses HIS gift of atonement to break HIS Torah, and then expects to be forgiven. As the Leshem continues to explain, it just doesn't work.

I have said something similar regarding the matter of what they said in Midrash Shir HaShirim, Ch. 1, on the verse, "With My...

steeds,"[1] Siman 6: "The Jewish people offered two Continual Offerings each day, one in the morning and one in the afternoon. The one in the morning was offered (which means it atoned, as in Bamidbar Rabbah, Parashas Pinchas, Siman 21) for sins that occurred during the night, and the one in the afternoon was offered (that is, atoned) for sins performed during the day. Thus, no one in Jerusalem slept with a sin, as it says, "Righteousness lodged in her" (Yeshayahu 1:21).

Part of the daily Temple service was to bring a Continual Offering—Korban Tamid—first thing in the morning, which atoned for any sins committed by the Jewish people the night before, and one in the late afternoon, to atone for sins committed since the morning Tamid.

Since this happened seven days a week, 365 days a year, the Jewish people had continuous atonement. There was never a day, or time of day, when they did not atone for sins committed. But what went wrong?

---

[1] The full verse is "With My mighty steeds, who battled Pharaoh's riders, I revealed that you are My beloved" (Shir HaShirim 1:9).

This seems to raise a question. If this was so, that they were always sinless, how did it happen that the destruction [of the Temple] occurred?

Both Temples were destroyed because of the sins of the Jewish people. But how could enough sins ever accumulate to result in such national catastrophes if they continuously brought the twice-daily Korban Tamid? What did they do to arrest the daily atonement process?

It was also in the same way mentioned, that they made the Continual Offerings the reason to sin, relying upon them to fulfill the whims of their hearts. In such a manner, they certainly did not atone at all, because the Continual Offerings were not given so they could sin; they were given to atone for sin.

The generations leading up to the destruction of the Temples erred, thinking that they could sin at night, and that the Continual Offering would atone for them the next morning, or they could sin during the day, and the Continual Offering would atone for them that evening. Since this reasoning was faulty, the offerings didn't do what was expected, and therefore their sins went unatoned. Thus enough accumulated to eventually result in the loss of the Temples.

> As it says in I Shmuel, 15:22, "And Shmuel said, 'Has God desire in burnt offerings and peace offerings, as in obeying the voice of God? Behold, to obey is better than a peace offering, etc.'"

Shaul HaMelech had been commanded to wipe out the entire nation of Amalek, which he did except for their king, Agag. He kept Agag alive temporarily because Shaul wanted to offer animals from Amalek to God as thanks for the victory, something he could not do after every last Amaleki had been killed.[2]

Although he had meant well, Shaul HaMelech erred, and gravely. It cost him the right to be king, as Shmuel told him. He also pointed out that there's no value in a sacrifice, even if offered with the best of intentions, if it is brought at the cost of obedience to God.

Likewise, what value was there in daily Continual Offerings if brought to atone for sins committed because of them? On the contrary, it rendered the offerings ineffective, spiritually blem-

---

2 Rashi, Devarim 25:19.

ished.

> Regarding all this, like this example, they say (Bereishis Rabbah, Ch. 34) that evil people change the Trait of Mercy to the Trait of Judgment.

Evil people cause God to judge the nation strictly, as opposed to mercifully. The most obvious reason is constant sinning. Nevertheless, based upon the principle about promises for good, they should not be able to interfere with the fulfillment of such a promise.

However:

> The sacrifices are what invoke mercy and atonement. But when they are made the basis for sin, and they rely on the atonement of the sacrifices for their sins, then the sacrifices will not atone at all. It is this that turns the mercy into judgment,

The Leshem rarely repeats himself without adding something new. In this case he is using his explanation of the verses from Yirmiyahu to explain the Midrash more deeply. Evil people, the Leshem explains, turn mercy into judgment not just because they sin, but because they make the basis of the mercy—sacrifices—the reason to sin.

> Likewise Yom HaKippurim is for atonement, but when they make Yom Kippur the reason to sin, then Yom Kippur does not atone. This is the turning of mercy into judgment.

Yom Kippur was given to the Jewish people as a day of mercy. But that mercy is only available to people who sin without trying to outsmart the system, people who sincerely regret the sin, and then ask God for forgiveness. A person who relies on Yom Kippur to protect him from punishment not only loses God's sympathy, but also becomes subject to punishment in spite of Yom Kippur.

> Likewise, every word that comes from the mouth of the Holy One, blessed is He, for good does not change even for sin, except when they make the promise the reason for the sin, relying on the promise to [excuse the] sin. Then they change the mercy to judgement, and the promise as well. This is what it is says in Yirmiyahu 18, "One moment I may speak concerning a nation or a kingdom, to build and establish [it], but if they do what is wrong in My eyes...I relent of the good, etc." Because in this way they make the promise

the reason to sin, and turn the mercy into judgment. They themselves make the sweet bitter and the good evil. However, all this is only when they sin because of the promise itself, that they relied on it, as mentioned. But other than this they do not change a single promise for good even because of sin. This is as it says in Tanchuma, Parashas Vayaira, Siman 13, and the Talmud, Shabbos 55a, that a good measure does not leave the mouth of the Holy One, blessed is He, and become retracted for evil, except for this; see there.

The Talmud is discussing what happened to the nation at the time of the destruction of the First Temple. This is the story:

[At the time of the destruction of the First Temple] the Holy One, blessed is He, told Gavriel,[3] "Go and make a mark of ink upon the foreheads of the righteous so that the Damaging Angel cannot harm them, and a mark of blood on the foreheads of the evil so

---

[3] This is the verse: "And God said to him, "Pass through the midst of the city, through the midst of Jerusalem, and you shall mark a sign upon the foreheads of the men who are sighing and moaning over all the abominations that were done in its midst" (Yechezkel 9:4).

that the Damaging Angel can harm them."

The Attribute of Judgment said before the Holy One, blessed is He, "Master of the universe, What difference is there between the two?"

He told it, "These were completely righteous, and these were completely evil."

It said before Him, "Master of the universe, they[4] could have protested, and didn't?"

He answered it, "It is revealed and known before Me that had they protested, they would not have been listened to!"

It answered Him, "To you it was revealed... but who revealed it to them?" (Shabbos 55a)

The Talmud concludes that God accepted the argument of the Attribute of Judgment, and consequently allowed both the evil and righteous to die alike. Thus, the good that God first spoke to spare the righteous was retracted, and the Damaging Angel was able to kill them as well.

Although, as the Talmud states, this was the only exception to the rule, in truth it shouldn't have been an exception at all. The Leshem therefore adds:

---

4 The righteous.

In truth, even in that case it is not relevant to call it a retraction per se, because it occurred at the actual time, while still involving the same matter. The Attribute of Justice prevented it, as clarified there. See there. This is not actually called a retraction.

In other words, the measure of good never had a chance to get off the ground. On the contrary, it was while God was actually making the promise for good that the Attribute of Justice stepped in and voiced its objection. It started off as a measure of good, but ended up being a measure of bad. So even in this case, a promise of good was not rescinded, and the principle still holds true.

This is certainly important to know today. An integral part of the Final Redemption picture is the return of the Jewish people to Eretz Yisroel, and the reestablishment of the Jewish State. Remarkably, after thousands of years of exile and little means to make it happen, this has nevertheless occurred.

Or has it?

Many believe not, since it has occurred through the hands of Jews who not only do not obey Torah, but who may not even believe in God. In fact much of the funding has come from Jews in the Diaspora who are secular, and even at the cost of Shabbos halachah. How, many have asked over the decades, can the fulfillment of ancient prophecies of redemption come true through people who disbelieve the very source of such prophecies?

The answer is clearer now. The promises are the promises, and they WILL be fulfilled regardless of the sins being committed at the time, as long as the promises are not the basis of the sins. Every Jew who disregards Torah law on any level will have to personally answer to God for it, Who takes into account what a person could or could not have known. Personal and even national culpability is His call and HIS call alone.

In the meantime, promises of redemption were made by God, Who already had knowledge of what the Jewish people would look like when their time for fulfillment would actually arrive. For our part, we have to trust that God will make good on His promises, and prepare ourselves for their inevitable fulfillment, making sure to be in the right place at the right time.

A search for trust

ten

Ya'akov's Story

JEWISH HISTORY IS anything BUT straightforward, at least on a simple level. It is constantly evolving and revealing information that only in the future makes the past clearer and more understandable. Until then, many questions will arise and many will remain unanswered, leaving plenty of room to have faith in God for what has already happened and to trust Him for what will continue to happen.

They say regarding Ya'akov Avinu, a"h, that when he feared Eisav, it was because of his great holiness and humility; he did not believe in himself and that he was worthy of being saved from him, and he suspected that he had stumbled with some sin.

Rashi himself mentions this on the following verse:

I have become small from all the kindnesses and from all the truth that You have given to Your servant, for with my staff I crossed this Jordan, and now I have become two camps. (Bereishis 32:11)

My merits have diminished because of the kindnesses and the truth that You have given to me. Therefore I fear in case I have become sullied with sin since [the time that] You promised me, and it will cause me to be delivered into Eisav's hand. (Rashi)

We know about the importance of the trait of humility from the Torah itself, when it discusses Moshe Rabbeinu's accolades.[1] But there is a time and a place for everything, including humility, and the confrontation with Eisav was apparently not

---

[1] Bamidbar 12:3.

one of them:

> Nevertheless, it was not proper at all, since our rabbis take him to task for it, as mentioned earlier. Through the messengers and gift that he sent ahead of him, he instigated [Eisav] against him, like grabbing the ear of a dog. Eisav had been going his way, and the messengers caused him to detour and bring him out.

Even if Ya'akov Avinu hadn't been worried about his merits being used up through sin, he should not have started up with Eisav. How much more so should he have circumvented Eisav if he weren't sure about the extent of his divine protection. It was like relying on a miracle, which we are not supposed to do.[2]

It gets even worse:

> Through the gift and by humbling himself before Eisav, he made him his leader and put himself into great danger this way. They say in the holy Zohar, Vayishlach, 166a, that he endangered himself. All the heavenly angels left him, Ya'akov was left alone (see the Mik-

---

[2] Shabbos 32a.

dosh Melech there), "and a man wrestled with him...he touched the socket of his hip" (Bereishis 32:25-26).

In order to return home from Padan Aram, Ya'akov and his entire entourage had to cross the Yabok River, a northern tributary of the Jordan River. By the end of the day, everything was on the other side, except for Ya'akov himself, who was attacked by an angel, the Angel of Eisav. His aloneness just seems to have been the result of moving everyone else to the other side of the river.

The Zohar, however, sees greater significance in Ya'akov's being alone. It didn't just happen by chance, but rather Ya'akov ended up alone because the angels who had accompanied him that far, and should still have been with him, had left. Apparently his instigation of Eisav caused this to happen, and the danger that resulted was not just for Ya'akov Avinu, but also for generations of righteous Jews yet to be born.

> They say in Bereishis Rabbah, at the end of Ch. 77, that he (i.e., the Angel of Eisav) "touched" righteous men and women, and male and female prophets. This refers to the generation of "Shmad."

The episode of Ya'akov Avinu's fight is quick and bizarre. At first it seems as if he were suddenly accosted by a bandit, which was far from unusual at that time. That they fought for hours is unusual. Also unusual was that Ya'akov, after defeating his assailant, just let him go as if nothing significant had happened, and even asked his would-be murderer for a blessing upon his departure!

The Torah doesn't make a big deal about any of this, but the Midrash and Zohar do. First, we are informed that the attacker had been none other than the Satan, the ministering angel of Eisav. This alone elevated the wrestling match to a heavenly struggle.

In general, everything the Avos did had direct implications for future generations, but this event did so in particular. The "night" itself was representative of the future exiles the Jewish people would have to endure. Victory at sunrise symbolized the Jewish people's eventual triumph and the Messianic Era destined to follow.

The fight to the death was more spiritual than physical. The Zohar says that the angel wanted to uproot Torah from the Jewish people altogether by damaging Ya'akov's body, because he specifically represented Torah. But "when he saw that he could not prevail against him" (Bereishis

32:26), he went after Ya'akov's leg instead.

Where and what the angel damaged is also kabbalistically and historically significant. The legs support the torso, and damaging Ya'akov's leg meant weakening the supporters of Torah. As the mishnah says, "If there is no flour, there is no Torah,"[3] and undermining future financial support of Torah learning was the angel's attempt to indirectly accomplish what he failed to do directly.

But that is not all the angel's "touch" undermined. Apparently the long-term damage the angel set in motion by causing Ya'akov's sciatic nerve to jump was physically catastrophic as well. It resulted in one of the darkest periods of Jewish history, called "Shmad—Destruction," when the Romans murdered righteous Jews wholesale, filling the streets with Jewish blood.[4]

> This effort of Ya'akov Avinu, a"h, [to appease his brother] caused all the evils and trouble of all the four exiles, as mentioned previously from Bereishis Rabbah Ch. 75, Siman 3, and Pirkei d'Rebi Eliezer, at the end of Ch. 37.

Thousands of years of history, many of them

---

[3] Pirkei Avos 3:21.
[4] Gittin 56b-58a.

filled with TERRIBLE suffering, are alluded to in only a FEW verses, and quite NONCHALANTLY. If not for the Midrash, it would be impossible to make the connection between what happened to Ya'akov Avinu one fateful night on his way home, and what has happened to his descendants during the four exiles that later followed.

However, after all is said and done, God forbid, Ya'akov Avinu, a"h, should not be faulted for any of this. He was the "chosen" of the Avos and all his ways and actions were always holy to God.

In everyday life, the actions of two people can SEEM exactly the same, until the intention of each is revealed or the circumstances that led each person to act as he did are made known. This can make the actions of one VERY different from that of the other.

Until this point the Leshem has presented Ya'akov Avinu's plan and execution as deliberate but mistaken. It may have been his extreme humility that led him to act as he did, but still, he carried it too far. If someone on Ya'akov Avinu's level could allow his fear of harm to interfere with his bitachon, then how could far lesser people be expected to act differently?

The Leshem explains. Ya'akov Avinu was not only great—he was extraordinary. To begin with, he was the third of the three Avos, the culmination of spiritual greatness that had been developed and honed by his father and grandfather. "Yeridas HaDoros," the spiritual weakening of following generations, did not apply to the period of the Avos themselves.

Rather, the Leshem now explains, there was something else going on behind the scenes that drove Ya'akov to act as he did, and which led to the consequences that resulted. Ya'akov Avinu's actions can only be properly understood within this context.

> Rather all that happened to him, all of it was "m'emek Chevron"...

This expression comes from a verse about Yosef's search for his brothers, as Rashi explains, after Ya'akov told him:

> "Go now and see to your brothers' welfare and the welfare of the flocks, and bring me back word." So he sent him from the valley of Chevron, and he came to Shechem. (Bereishis 37:14)

But is not Chevron on a mountain? It says: "And they ascended in the south, and he came as far as Chevron" (Bamidbar 13:22). Rather [Ya'akov sent Yosef] from the deep counsel of the righteous man who is buried in Chevron (i.e., Avraham) to fulfill what was said to Avraham "bein habesarim—between the parts" [as it says], "Your progeny will be strangers" (Bereishis 15:13). (Rashi)

In the verse, "m'emek Chevron" is just a physical location. As Rashi points out, however, it alludes to the pact made between God and Avraham, and all that it was destined to entail:

…to fulfill the profound decree that the Holy One, blessed is He, established between Him and that righteous person buried in Chevron.

In other words, everything that happened to Ya'akov Avinu was part of the fulfillment of the covenant established between God and Avraham Avinu, all part of the "Bris Bein HaBesarim—Covenant Between the Halves."

This certainly explains many of the strange goings-on that happened throughout the story. For example, did Ya'akov Avinu, one of the greatest prophets who ever lived, not know what just about every average parent knows about not fa-voring one child over another?[5] Of course he did.

And when he sent Yosef to check on his brothers, did Ya'akov Avinu not realize that he was endangering Yosef? How could he not know, after seeing how his other sons felt about Yosef? Ya'akov may have been pure, but he wasn't naive.

The Midrash puts all this into perspective. It says that Ya'akov was MADE to favor Yosef so that his brothers WOULD become jealous of him, and WOULD sell him into slavery. It was all necessary to set in motion the events destined to occur be-cause of the Bris Ben HaBesarim,[6] which was about a LOT more than just a promise of future good and prophecy of future exile.

> It was the vision of the Ben HaBesarim, and it says there that "a great darkness was falling upon him" (Bereishis 15:12). The Holy One, blessed is He, showed him the four kingdoms, it says in the Midrash there, Ch. 44, Siman 17. This was the basis of all that happened to Ya'akov with Eisav, according to which the "actions of the fathers are a sign for the chil-dren," as the Ramban writes in Parashas Lech

---

[5] Shabbos 10b.

[6] Tanchuma, Vayaishev 4.

Lecha 12:6, and in Parashas Vayishlach.

There were two major things that made the Avos unique. First, there was their level of spiritual greatness. Their capacity to sense and relate to God was extraordinary and defies imagination. They epitomized the idea of spiritual beings having physical experiences, which is why their every waking moment was devoted to the service of God.

The second aspect was the time frame in which the Avos lived. History is composed of many periods, and one is not similar to another, neither in opportunity nor impact. In these two respects, the period of the Avos was one of the most unique of all,[7] and they fully understood this.

This is what gives rise to the idea that "ma'aseh Avos siman l'banim—actions of the fathers are a sign for the children." It doesn't just mean that what the Avos did are good examples to follow, although it certainly means this as well. It means that when the Avos did something with historic significance, it had impact on the destiny of their descendants.

Through their decisions and actions, the Avos

_____

[7] Derech Hashem 2:4:3.

steered Jewish history. They did whatever they could in THEIR lifetimes to light the way for all the generations to follow them until Yemos HaMoshiach. But as can be seen from the Bris Bein HaBesarim and the thousands of years of history that followed, there was only so much they could do to mitigate future circumstances.

However, there is a missing piece of information. It's only alluded to in the Talmud, and not really discussed much by the Midrash. It belongs to the realm of Kabbalah, even though it is the driving force behind ALL of history, even and ESPECIALLY the suffering.

It has to do not so much with history SINCE Creation, but what happened before it, on the way to making a world that could support free will, and therefore the reality of evil as well. Creation is "broken," and man was created to use his free will to fix it.

There are a number of ways to rectify Creation. Torah and mitzvos are the preferred way, which is why the yetzer hara fights so strongly against them. People think that they're too smart to believe in Torah, or too free to be bound by mitzvos. In fact they have just been conned by their yetzer haras, and left in the crosshairs of divine retribution in the next world and quite possibly in this world as well.

The yetzer hara doesn't necessarily have to stop all learning of Torah, although he would love to, in order to accomplish his goal. He just needs to weaken Torah learning and mitzvah performance enough to put the rectification of Creation behind the divine schedule. God will then take care of the rest, making up for "lost" time through exile and all its attendant sufferings.

> The fear that Ya'akov felt in his heart was from what was written with respect to Avraham Avinu, a"h, "a great darkness was falling upon him." He showed him all the bitter exiles and terrible suffering the Jewish people would have to endure from Eisav until the coming of Moshiach.

This is what Ya'akov saw when he looked at Eisav. He didn't just see a vengeful man who could murder his own brother in cold blood without a smidgen of guilt. He saw the ancestor of countless future nations who would do the same to his descendants for thousands of years to come, until Moshiach will finally put history back on track.

That's what Ya'akov Avinu saw, and so much more. Even though we are on the other side of history now, having lived through what he could only dread, we still lack his complete vision. We tend to think in immediate terms, and worry only about our OWN future. Ya'akov Avinu saw beyond even our time frame, and far deeper into Creation.

Ya'akov Avinu understood on the deepest of levels what was broken in Creation, and what needed to occur in order to fix it. He did what he could, like his father and grandfather before him, to leave us the necessary tools to finish what they had started. His personal journey was planned in order to do exactly that. That's why he even tried to reveal the End-of-Days to us.[8]

But at the end of the day, the most important tool he COULD leave us to survive history, and accomplish the most with our opportunities at life, remains to be a our most valuable asset: bitachon, trust in God. And the reason for this is also quite kabbalistic.

---

[8] Bereishis 49:1.

A search for trust

eleven

Bridge of Knowing

ONE OF THE problems that people have with the idea of bitachon is that it just seems so passive. They can see that trust is the basis of every good relationship, but when it comes to relying on something for survival, they prefer something more proactive, and participatory. This gives them a greater sense of something actually being done to solve their problem.

Like prayer, for example. At least prayer is something you actually DO, and it has a known and understandable process and potential impact. Bitachon you just…HAVE, and how can just

HAVING something result in any kind of DRA-MATIC effect?

This is a good question, until we understand how Creation ACTUALLY works. We live in a very physical world, one that is quite ACTION-oriented. For the most part, things only SEEM to get accomplished after something is PHYSICALLY done. Doing nothing PHYSICAL and only TRUSTING God to succeed at something is, for many, a last-resort approach, once all else has failed.

But as powerful as prayer is, and it is VERY powerful, its words can reach only SO high, and do only SO much. It's the way the "system" was built, the way the world was made. The PHYSICAL world we know best is but a VERY small fraction of ALL of Creation. It is the SPIRITUAL world within and beyond the physical one that is vaster beyond imagination.[1]

Consequently, physical action is spiritually "heavy," and its ability to ascend and influence outcomes is therefore limited. Should a person pray halachically correctly, his words will still stall at a certain height in the spiritual system of the flow of divine light. If he prays less than perfectly, they may barely ascend at all.

What CAN ascend higher, even all the way to

---

[1] Drushei Olam HaTohu, Chelek 2, Drush 5, Anaf 4, Siman 7.

the "top" of the system is the spiritual component of prayer, the intention—KAVANAH—with which a person has imbued his words. As the words of prayer fall back to earth like a rocket booster, so to speak, it's the person's kavanah that has the potential to continue on to a more ultimate destination.[2]

Bitachon is a kavanah. It's an intention. It is a way of thinking, a way of looking at the world. As such, it is something that has to be LEARNED and DEVELOPED. We're born with muscles, but their potential strength is only actualized with exercise. We're born with an ability to trust in God, for EVERYTHING. But only by exercising this trust over time can we just HAVE it, especially when we need it the most.

This is one reason why bitachon is NOT passive. A lot of effort is required to understand and strengthen it. Becoming a "ba'al bitachon," a master of bitachon, takes a lifetime, and a LOT of time and energy. And given the nature of the yetzer hara to make us panic at a time of crisis, it takes a lot of will power to stay with bitachon when a sit-

---

[2] Rockets use powerful boosters to overcome the earth's gravitational pull and bring the main capsule into space. Once the boosters go as far as they can, their fuel spent, they are jettisoned and fall back to earth, allowing the capsule to continue the journey to its intended destination.

uation looks dire.

Another reason bitachon requires effort is due to how it works. It's a spiritual bridge builder. God made the world above and the one below. But He left the connecting piece between them for man to create and maintain through his free-will decisions.

Everything the world below could ever want, and then some, exists in the world above. We could NEVER inventory what is stored up there, but we can also never access it without that bridge. And like any bridge, its ability to support "traffic" will depend upon what the bridge is made from, and whether it exists at all.

Like all construction, it's possible to cut corners and use shoddy materials. You can still end up with a bridge, but not one that will last very long or hold much weight. More than likely, it will collapse just when needed most, and with many casualties.

When it comes to constructing the bridge between heaven and earth, the best material is bitachon. We see it down here on earth in our relationships with people. Nothing bonds a couple more than mutual trust. The more "bitachon" exists between people, the more they become one with each other.

It's not something that gives results overnight. Trust by definition requires time and effort, because time and effort are what it takes to know another person really well, and they are the KEY ingredients to any trust relationship. No one EVER trusts a stranger for anything important, unless he has no choice, and even then he will worry about the result.

This is the reason people have such difficulty with bitachon. It's not the idea that bothers them, but rather the "stranger." They don't KNOW God very well, and yet they're being advised to TRUST Him…for EVERYTHING. No wonder they only do it, if at all, as a LAST resort.

We NEED the bridge. It may seem optional, but it is not. Unfortunately, except in certain rare instances, this is not something people can appreciate until AFTER they have built the bridge, or are at least well on their way. It takes emunah, faith, to get started.

This, essentially, is what God told the Jewish people when He said:

> You have been SHOWN, in order to KNOW that God, He is God; there is none else besides Him. (Devarim 4:35)

That is where the Avos really excelled. They KNEW God exceptionally well. They had no problem trusting Him with everything that mattered to them because they knew God well enough to trust Him to such an extent. Trusting God was the most obvious and natural thing to do for them, once they knew Him on the level they did.

The same is true of Moshe Rabbeinu, as the Talmud implies:

> Rebi Chanina further said: "Everything is in the hand of heaven except the fear of heaven, as it says, 'And now, Israel, what does God, your God, require of you but to fear, etc.?' (Devarim 10:12)."
>
> "Is fear of heaven such a small thing? Didn't Rebi Chanina say in the name of Rebi Shimon bar Yochai, 'The Holy One, blessed is He, has nothing in His treasury except a store of fear of heaven,' as it says, 'The fear of God is His treasure'"? (Yeshayahu 33:6)
>
> "Yes, for Moshe it was a small thing, as Rebi Chanina said, 'A parable is if a man is asked for a big article. If he has it, it seems like a small article to him. But if he is asked for a small article and he does not have it, then it seems like a big article to him.'" (Brochos 33b)

Moshe Rabbeinu didn't have enormous fear of God just because he just CHOSE to. He had it because of his intimate knowledge of God. He spoke to God "face to face," which means that he was extremely close to God. God called him the most trustworthy in His house.[3] He was, after all, the greatest prophet to have EVER lived.[4] MOSHE RABBEINU'S awe of God was accurate. OURS is not even in the ballpark.

Therefore, the bridge of bitachon is built from knowledge of God. The Rambam says this outright:

> Regarding the Almighty, the glorious, and the awesome One, it is a mitzvah to love and fear Him, as it says, "And you shall love God, your God" (Devarim 6:5) and "You must fear God, your God" (Devarim 6:13). What is the way to love Him and to fear Him? Once a person meditates on His actions and His awesome and great creations, and observes His wisdom, that it is without estimable value or limit, immediately he will love, praise, glorify, and greatly desire to know His great name, as Dovid said, "My soul thirsts for God, the living God" (Tehillim 42:3). (Yad, Hilchos Yesodei Ha-Torah, 2:1-2)

---

[3] Bamidbar 12:6-8.
[4] Devarim 34:10.

To KNOW God is to LOVE Him. To KNOW God is to FEAR Him. And to KNOW God is to TRUST Him. To KNOW Him is to build a bridge between heaven and earth so that divine light can flow freely from the Trusted to the one who trusts.

This is why the Midrash can guarantee that nothing stands in the way of bitachon. Why should it? The solution already exists in heaven. The need for it exists on earth. And if a person has made the effort and taken the time to know God well enough, the bridge between the two exists as well, allowing for the flow of divine light and blessing to continue to the person unabated. "The system is full proof," God tells us. "Trust Me."

THE FOLLOWING TITLES are all the books written over the years. Some books may no longer be in print, but many are still available in either PDF or Kindle formats. Visit the Thirtysix.org OnLine Bookstore, or Amazon for more information, or to order online.

If you order using AmazonSmile, each purchase will generate a contribution for Thirtysix.org. You just have to designate "Thirtysix Org Inc." as your charitable organization of choice, and Amazon will take care of the rest.

The Unbroken Chain of Jewish Tradition, 1985
The Eternal Link, 1990
If Only I Were Wealthy, 1992
If Only I Understood Why, 1993
If Only I Could See the Forest, 1993
If Only I Could Stay, 1993

If Only Great Was Greater, 1993
The Y Factor, 1994
Life's A Thrill, 1994
No Atheists in a Foxhole, 1994
Changes that Last Forever, 1994
The Making of a Great Jewish Leader, 1994
Bereishis: A Beginning With No End, 1994
The Wonderful World of Thirtysix, 1995
Redemption to Redemption, 1997
The Big Picture, 1998
Perceptions, 1998
Not Just Another Scenario, 2001
At The Threshold, 2001
Anticipating Redemption, 2002
Sha'ar HaGilgulim, 2002
Hadran, 2004
Talking About The End of Days, 2005
Talking About Eretz Yisroel, 2005
The Physics of Kabbalah, 2006
Be Positive, 2007
Geulah b'Rachamim, 2007
God.calm, 2007
Just Passing Through, 2007
On The Same Page, 2007
The Equation of Life, 2007
No Such Victim, 2009
Survival in 10 Easy Steps, 2009
Not Just Another Scenario 2, 2011

All In Your Mind, 2011
The Light of Thirtysix, 2011
The Last Exile, 2011
Drowning in Pshat, 2012
Drown No More, 2012
Shas Man, 2013
The Mystery of Jewish History, 2013
Survival Guide For the End-of-Days, 2013
Deeper Perceptions, 2013
Chanukah Lite, 2015
The Hitchhiker's Guide to Armageddon, 2016
Purim Lite, 2016
Pesach Lite, 2016
The Torah Empowerment Seminar, 2016
Siman Tov, 2016
The Fabric of Reality, 2016
Addendum, 2016
Fundamentals of Reincarnation, 2017
Reincarnation Clarified, 2016
All About Energy, 2017
What Goes Around, 2017
The God Experience, 2017
What in Heaven, 2017
The God Experience, Part 2, 2017
The God Experience, Part 3, 2017
It's About Time, 2017
Need to Know, 2017
Perceptions, Volume 2, 2017

Once Revealed, Twice Concealed, 2017
The Art of Chayn, 2017
A Matter of Laugh or Death, 2018
Geulah b'Rachamim Program, V. 1, 2018
Geulah b'Rachamim Program, V. 2, 2018
Geulah b'Rachamim Program, V. 3, 2018
Point of Acceptance, 2018
See Ya, 2018
In Discussion: Bereishis, 2018
Reincarnation Again, 2018
A Separate Matter, 2018
In Discussion: Shemos, 2019
A Search for Self, 2019
A Search for Trust, 2019

For more information regarding any of these books or other projects, write to pinchasw@thirtysix.org, especially if you are interested in making a dedication in an upcoming publication.

essays, books, video, audio that which change the way you look at life—and history